Lazy Virtues

Lazy Virtues

Teaching Writing
in the Age of Wikipedia

Robert E. Cummings

Vanderbilt University Press • Nashville

13 12 11 10 09   1 2 3 4 5

This book is printed on acid-free paper.
Manufactured in the United States of America

Library of Congress Cataloging-in-Publication Data

Cummings, Robert E., 1967–
Lazy virtues : teaching writing in the age of Wikipedia / Robert E.
Cummings.
p. cm.
Includes bibliographical references and index.
ISBN 978-0-8265-1615-2 (cloth: alk. paper)
ISBN 978-0-8265-1616-9 (pbk. : alk. paper)
1. English language—Rhetoric—Study and teaching (Higher)
2. Academic writing—Study and teaching (Higher)
3. Internet in education. 4. Internet publishing. 5. Wikipedia
I. Title.
PE1404.C87 2008
808'.042071—dc22
2008022130

This book is dedicated to Jack,
who saw me all the way home.
Rest in peace, my loyal friend.

Contents

Acknowledgments

I give many thanks to Anita DeRouen, who helped me so much in conducting the focus group surveys. I owe a debt of gratitude to Christy Desmet for being such a patient mentor and telling me what I needed to hear—always in no uncertain terms. Steve Ramsay has my thanks for being a man who not only embodies an amazing passion to share cool ideas but also has a lot of them to share (for him, I trust this book became something more than "Wikis, rah-rah!"). I thank Ron Miller for backing me when no one else would. I remain grateful to Cindy Selfe for her immediate and enthusiastic support of this project, and her willingness to serve on my committee—though it never came to pass—and her great service to the computers and writing community. Betsy Phillips at Vanderbilt University Press also showed immediate enthusiasm for this text and supported me throughout the process of seeing it to print. Ron Balthazor remains my inspiration for embodying the ideal: a great passion for the humanities with as great a knowledge of coding, and a spiritual patience to supply equal servings to the frantic masses. I thank Nelson Hilton for visionary department chairmanship, and his acerbic agreement with De Gaulle that graveyards are indeed filled with indispensable men. Alexis Hart has been, for all who know her, a great inspiration, and she certainly was for me during the starting days of this project. I'd like to thank Charlie Lowe for providing valuable criticism of an earlier draft of this work. I credit Jay Watson with helping me prepare for this day by serving, years ago, as my advisor.

But if there is any credit to be claimed for the production of this text, it goes to my wife, Beth, for whom every page here represents a personal sacrifice and a page unwritten in her own work. The blame, as always, is entirely my own.

Introduction

Having picked up this book, there is a good chance you have heard of Wikipedia. And if you know anything about Wikipedia, chances are also strong that you fall into one of two groups: you are either curious about Wikipedia and want to learn more, or you are worried by it—or a particular aspect of it—and are looking for confirmation of those worries. (The group of people who picked up this book because they are excited about Wikipedia and think it is a good development is, alas, still small enough to gloss over for the moment.) This book is not an orientation to Wikipedia newcomers (though indeed it contains a good amount of information about Wikipedia and practical guidance on its use in the writing classroom), nor is it a tract on the evils of Wikipedia with the inevitable accompanying lament on the fall of standards and credibility associated with the waning of print culture. Rather, it is dedicated to understanding what Wikipedia represents in terms of higher education, making knowledge, and teaching writing. It sees Wikipedia not only as a particular instance of a wiki but also as a harbinger of a new way of writing—and a new way of working. This text aims to give practical advice to teachers of writing who wish to explore collaborative electronic platforms in the composition classroom. But, more important, in evaluating that type of composition environment, it reveals new and useful thinking about how knowledge production in the higher-education classroom arrived where it is today and how it will need to shift to best accommodate our students' needs.

I have a friend, John Kasay, who was an assistant coach of football at the University of Georgia through the 1980s and during much of the glory that followed their 1980 national championship with Herschel Walker. Every summer, football programs in America—professional, college, high school, and on down—hold practice in the scorching summer sun. Conventional coaching wisdom during most of John's career held that the staff should deny players access to water during those practice sessions because it toughened the players. This line of thinking infuriated John. When I asked him why, thinking that perhaps he was angered by the endangerment of the players' health through dehydration, he surprised me with an even more direct logic. He asked, "On game day, how much water do the players get?" I thought. "All they want?" "Exactly," replied John. "Train your players for the environment in which they will perform." Though he was indeed concerned about player dehydration as well, John felt the old method of denying water to players during practice did not merit evaluation based on ethics alone. It made no sense in terms of strategy. John's thinking reveals a clear logic about the connection between preparation and performance.

The traditional role of academics is to prepare students for contemporary society through a broad liberal arts curriculum. We teach pure mathematics, comparison-and-contrast essay writing, Latin grammar, and sculpture not because our graduates will be asked to write integrals that allow the comparison, in Latin, of the relative merits of two sculptures, and not only because these activities do indeed have some residual cultural capital, but because they teach our students how to think. If the advent of Wikipedia marks a change in the future world in which our students will work, a liberal arts curriculum provides the best strategy for preparing them for it. Unlike a technical preparation, which relies on the specifics of contemporary tools, a liberal arts preparation does not base its curriculum on the particulars of the current technology but provides the training to evaluate any particular instance of technology by understanding how it affects knowledge creation itself.

My particular domain within that liberal arts curriculum is the first-year composition class. John's comments caused me to rethink just how great the disconnect between first-year composition pedagogy and my students' future writing lives had become. For years I had watched and even participated in the fairly standard approach of teaching first-year composition by choosing readings that interested me out of, say, *Everything's an Argument*, and building writing assignments around them. These essays were designed to reach sound composition outcomes: the development of critical thinking, the creation of awareness of the modes of composition, the interpretation of evidence, the citation of sources, and the establishment of main ideas. But as my graduate school career progressed, I became more involved in Humanities Computing. One day in 2002, I stumbled across an emerging Wikipedia, and immediately saw it as a challenge to the singularity of the current knowledge production paradigm of higher education; what I did not see until much later is how it could also become a teaching tool, by providing my writing students with a genuine audience.

There are no shortages of persuasive and alarming predictions about the future of literacy in our students' lives. Doubtless you too have sat through PowerPoints that presented no end of startling facts to raise anxiety, fear, and doubt about the future, and heighten our inadequacies as we try to educate students to thrive in such a rapidly changing world. Thus it was with great joy that I found the writings of Yochai Benkler. The insights in Benkler's article "Coase's Penguin, or Linux and the Nature of the Firm" (2002) provided a logical and clear framework to understand the knowledge production system of Wikipedia. Further, "Coase's Penguin" also informed me with a better understanding of how the composition classroom had become structured around certain fundamental assumptions about literacy and the academic publishing model, none of which appeared to be particularly applicable to current practices. "Coase's Penguin" and Benkler's later work *The Wealth of Networks* helped me to understand the development of composition practices—oddly enough—in terms of economic practices, revealing how forces typically excluded from our analyses of the discipline's approaches had shaped our assumptions about teaching. This understanding allows for a sense of direction—if not outright relief—in the face of the ever-welling anxiety fueled by those PowerPoint literacy factoids. The goal of this work, then, is to share that knowledge, guidance, and concomitant sense of direction, through six major concepts about the teaching of writing developed herein.

Writing for Wikipedia included direct engagement with the Wikipedians themselves. A persistent question in the back of my mind, as well as my students' minds, had been "Who are these people?" Who has the time, interest, and expertise to develop lengthy articles and then perpetually police them against vandals? (Or sloppy, unmotivated college writing?) More difficult still, who then evaluates new contributions and integrates them into existing articles? In answering this question, I came back to a concept I had studied in Humanities Computing that explained why computer programming enthusiasts had collaborated to develop the operating system Linux. It had become known to me, eventually, as "laziness."

"Laziness" had been first described to me in the context of the hacker community's preference for repurposing existing code for new tasks rather than writing entirely new code. Hacking (not to be confused with the often criminal pursuit of "cracking") is really the idea of taking an object designed for one purpose, modifying it, and then applying it to another context entirely. But "laziness" also incorporated another idea from the hacker community, that of working on projects simply for the enjoyment of learning something new, seeing jobs done well, and/or earning recognition for skillful work. Hacker culture, born of the network relationships so accurately predicted by Manuel Castells (2000), also acknowledged that working collaboratively on nonlinear, granularized projects allowed (and maybe even required) a rethinking of the traditional work environment, which had sprung up to support labor completed for more traditional motivations. If people were now working for their own satisfaction, on their own time, and perhaps in their own homes, "laziness" seemed also to catch up the core idea of working closer to one's true interests, representing a work environment that encouraged spontaneity, individuality, and creativity.

There is little coincidence that these values described as "laziness" are at odds with the inherent value of "work," so often tied to Max Weber's *Protestant Ethic and the Spirit of Capitalism*. Since, in an electronic environment, existing work products can often be reproduced without charge, the originality and creativity of contributors are paramount. These are not a bad set of factors for writers. Working without traditional pay is what binds the new knowledge community on Wikipedia. Thus, this text is centered around the development and application of six key concepts for the composition classroom:

- **Commons-based peer production (CBPP)**. Benkler identifies CBPP as a new economic mode of production, adding it to market mode (working by one's self for the marketplace) and firm mode (working together under management). CBPP occurs when the costs of collaboration are extremely low and the nature of the work at hand is amenable to distribution over a network such as the Internet. For the writing classroom, CBPP means maximizing the value added to collaborative projects and maximizing student autonomy (and thus capability) by allowing writers to select projects or topics based on their interests.
- **Authenticity**. If there is staleness in the composition classroom, it is often found in students' views of their audience. Most assignments ask writers to imagine an audience—and then to compose for their composition instructor as a surrogate for that idealized, fictional audience. Walter Ong's notion that all audiences are fictional aside, CBPP and wiki assignments allow students to write for an authentic audience beyond the classroom. And, in the case of the Wikipedia writing assignments explored herein, these audiences often write back.
- **Professional Standards**. By asking students to produce work that attempts to satisfy real needs, teachers put them in positions where their writings have an undeniable impact. With CBPP writing assignments, students are challenged and motivated to produce writing with accurate and relevant content for larger projects external to the classroom. And for that content to be acknowledged by the professional community, it must be credible in terms of ethos, with a reasoned voice that reflects a sense of the values of that knowledge community.
- **Epistemology**. Writing for CBPP projects that report knowledge, especially Wikipedia, involves students in the process of creating and producing knowledge according to the standards of a field. To be sure, some knowledge communities distance themselves from the topic pages of Wikipedia, but whether or not the Wikipedia knowledge community is embraced beyond that site, it has its own rules for deciding what kinds of knowledge are accepted, what kinds of knowledge are under

review, and what kinds of knowledge are rejected. CBPP writing assignments develop epistemological awareness by asking students to participate in CBPP projects, to understand the accepted knowledge-making procedures for their project's community, and, when challenged, to reevaluate and defend their contributions according to the stated acceptable practices of that knowledge community.

- **Transition**. The approach to teaching college writing described herein also works well because it reinforces the transition from general knowledge to specific and authoritative knowledge that the college writer is undergoing. As aptly described in Keith Hjortshoj's *Transition to College Writing* (2001), the first-year college student is moving from an environment where teachers are largely generalists (high school) to an environment with teachers of increasing specialization (college). First-year composition plays a pivotal role in this transition toward greater specialization and expertise; as students get their bearings in the college environment, CBPP writing assignments assist them in understanding the role of producing knowledge for our culture rather than only consuming it.

- **Laziness**. The term "laziness" has been used to describe the computer coding belief that it is preferable to reuse code by copying it, rather than rewriting it or authoring it anew. In this text, "laziness" also refers to the larger concept of saving personal investment in work projects for those areas that require or emphasize individual creativity and might not render traditional rewards. Thus, "laziness" in the writing classroom does not involve "reusing" the text of other writers through plagiarism, but emphasizes instead that each writer should examine the project's overall needs and create his or her own contributions based on an awareness of the project's needs and one's own creative desires. "Laziness" describes the condition of striking a balance between what needs to be done and what one wants to do, framed by an awareness of what has already been done.

Readers might well wonder about the wisdom of basing a composition pedagogy on CBPP, a largely economic phenomenon. Is this Internet "cyber hype"? Will students really be affected by these developments in their future writing lives? How much impact will CBPP have on our larger culture?

To answer these concerns, readers need look no further than one of the largest problems facing our planet, and a creative (and possibly the most pragmatic) response to that problem. There can be little argument that global warming is a serious long-term concern facing our planet, but this difficult problem also serves as an instructive example of the commons concept. Usually, the idea of the commons is introduced not far from the phrase "the tragedy of the commons," meaning a resource that no one owns and from which everyone can benefit. Global warming is a "tragedy of the commons" problem, since there are no individual costs associated with carbon dioxide emissions; under the current system, it is in almost everyone's immediate financial interests to emit carbon dioxide, just as assuredly as it is to no one's long-term benefit.

The Vehicle Design Summit (VDS), one of the most creative solutions to this problem, employs the concept of the commons and serves as a prime example of the types of CBPP collaborations our students will find increasingly common. The VDS describes itself as follows: "Driven to develop a new class of automobile, the Vehicle Design Summit aims to create a 4-passenger, 200 MPGe, high-performance industry-standard car with minimal life cycle costs and wide appeal both in developed and developing countries. Building off of a 9-week 24/7 design program in summer 2006 (in which four driving prototypes were built from scratch by an all-volunteer team of 55 student engineers), VDS 2.0 is recruiting up to 35 teams of university students to collaboratively develop the 2.0 vehicle (codenamed Vision)" (VDS 2007).

The VDS is a defining example of student-led CBPP. To serve a common goal, tasks are subdivided and distributed globally, while coordination and collaboration are facilitated across the Internet. Speaking specifically to why students—as opposed to other groups—might naturally collaborate to tackle the world's toughest problems, the VDS webpage comments that "students are typically motivated by a blend of intellectual curiosity and passion for real-world tangible results developed in concert with other future industry leaders. University teams the world over already work on custom plug-in hybrids, super-mileage vehicles, solar racecars, formula cars and scores of other complex problem-solving endeavors. VDS proposes to create a meta-team drawing from the same creative drive that inspires such student teams to constructively compete. The eventual goal of VDS 2.0 is a single production-ready automobile developed in an open, collaborative environment" (VDS 2007). While CBPP might not spark collaborative projects of such a comprehensive nature in the composition classroom, certainly the VDS is evidence that CBPP itself is an increasingly common phenomenon.

Younger undergraduates often express frustration with their education, reporting a sense of disconnect between their college experience and their perceived application of that education. The professionals in their fields evidence a disciplinary knowledge of great specificity—perhaps in the practice of journalism, or in marine biology—that is exotic compared to writing essays in first-year composition or cutting open another frog boiled in formaldehyde. Students describe languishing in the boredom of their core curriculum—seen by them as repetitive of their high school curriculum and removed from "real world" applications—while anxiously awaiting the opportunity to apply themselves to upper-division courses where the "real" knowledge takes place. But this is no reason to do away with the core: students enter college with a wide variety of preparations, and our institutions have little choice but to prepare them for the applied activities of their majors by ensuring a common set of skills through the foundation of a core. But the students' dis-ease with "laboratory" knowledge of the core—contrasted with their enthusiasm for authentic professional application—is tangible. Applying knowledge to make a difference creates a sense of identity, and that too is why our students are in college. Beginning undergraduates often envy someone who can say with certainty, "I'm a psychologist" or "I'm a civil engineer." Outside of the academic counseling office, no one who says "I'm undeclared" feels a sense of place.

Writing for Wikipedia provides students with a more genuine audience. Although the heterogeneous audience of Wikipedia often comes with a new set of problems, more often than not they are writers bound together by an interest in and passion for a topic. Each Wikipedia entry forms its own knowledge community. On Wikipedia, writers are motivated to represent the state of knowledge on that topic in a uniformly readable way, and their passion for that task can often create an amazing marriage between expert knowledge and coherent communication (for a perpetually updated example, see the Wikipedia article on "Featured Content"). While the many examples of how Wikipedia has also failed to produce credible articles are all too familiar, it was stable enough to expose my students to the demands of producing writing for a professional knowledge community: a place where their writing would be read and evaluated for its accuracy, its relevance, and its efficiency. This not only solved the problem of connecting the "disconnected" core course of composition to a real, authentic knowledge community, it also helped take the teacher out of the position of audience. Writing teachers have long known that we cannot teach grammar and mechanics away from the context of a motivated writer with a clear understanding of audience, message, and purpose. Once writers care about making the audience understand something important, they are invested in spelling, punctuation, and style. Writing on wikis provided my students with that audience trigger. More importantly, the contents of their messages were judged by the community's standards. I saw that asking my students to write for the Wikipedia audience moved me out of the audience role, and also gave them a sense of how a highly engaged audience behaved—and maybe a sense of what awaited them once they graduated from college, lessening the disconnect between the core and the real world. Wikipedia was the water at football practice, bringing a game day sensibility to the classroom skill-building.

Over the next several chapters, then, this text will attempt to expand a rationale for introducing CBPP in the composition classroom, offer a practical guide for doing so, and explore the reasons for the development for such a phenomenon. There's no guarantee your writers will solve global warming, but your writing class will never be the same.

1

Commons-Based Peer Production and the Composition Classroom

Different technologies make different kinds of human interaction easier or harder to perform. All other things being equal, things that are easier to do are more likely to be done, and things that are harder to do are less likely to be done. All other things are never equal.
—Yochai Benkler (2006, 17)

The "Wickipedia" Epidemic: Signs of a Problem in Composition Studies

Seen on an English department electronic mailing list ("Wikipedia Epidemic" 2005):

Composition Instructor 1:
Is anyone else out there suffering from the WICKIPEDIA epidemic? Over half of my students in 1102M seem to have cited this highly unreliable source on their most recent paper. . . . Am I [a] staid stick-in-the-mud for being horrified by students' use of this source? Actually, I'm fascinated by it as a pop culture phenomenon, but I'm horrified by the all-too-democratic "best source for information" concept.

Composition Instructor 2:
While I'm not yet suffering from Wikipedia, I am suffering [from] an over reliance on the Internet. I encourage my students to avoid it, since

there is so much tripe published on the Internet as fact. . . . Use of
suspect sources may result in a reduction in their grade, as I consider it
part of the responsibility of instructors to teach them how to do proper
research for any topic that may be assigned while in college. If they
have to use electronic sources, please stick to [our library's subscription
database gateway], and remember that not everything there is valid. So
I guess I'm an old fuddy duddy myself.

Composition Instructor 3:
One thing I've done is schedule an electronic resource day with a
reference librarian to get all of them up to speed on using the library's
databases. . . . With all the resources of [our library's holdings
database] just a password away, they have little excuse to use a
Wikipedia.

Teachers of writing at the college level are confused as never before
about what they should be teaching their writers. Most of the confusion results from the impact of information technology—and, more
specifically, the Internet—on the lives of their students. These teachers
get little support and guidance from their institutions and mentors on
how to identify and respond to the changes of electronic communication; there is little consensus in the field of composition as to exactly
what teachers of writing need to understand about emergent technologies
in order to do their jobs. Both in popular culture and the media, new
forms of electronic writing such as blogs and wikis have recently gar-
nered a lot of attention, yet no one is sure exactly how to respond in the
classroom to these new forms of writing. If the teachers quoted are any
example, teachers of writing are still wrestling with issues of academic
authority initiated by the advent of the World Wide Web more than ten
years ago.

The technical definition of a wiki is, surprisingly, the simplest: A wiki
is a webpage users can modify. The earliest known wiki, the WikiWiki-
Web project, was envisioned essentially as a software development tool; it
started on May 1, 1995, when a software programmer named Ward Cunningham posted a note to a developers' electronic mailing list (*c2.com/cgi/
wiki?InvitationToThePatternsList*). Cunningham had developed a database
to collect the contributions of the mailing list's members. He had noticed

that the content of the list tended to get buried, and therefore the most recent poster might be ignorant of posts preceding his or hers.

A wiki is a software piece that combines the contemporaneous focus of an electronic mailing list with the data storage capabilities of a database. It is an electronic mailing list with a memory. Knowing these details, however, does not capture the full dynamic of writing in a wiki; even experienced writing teachers will find that contemporary electronic writing environments present challenges to their conceptualization of the writing classroom. There can be little doubt that wikis are already a part of their students' writing experiences. Writing teachers know they are training students to write in a landscape that, if the last decade serves as any indicator, will probably be radically transformed by as yet unforeseen aspects of electronic literacy.

These teachers do not need another book on hypertext or new media theory. What they do need is an overview of which particular aspects of the ever-evolving information technology field have the greatest potential to impact the lives of their students as writers. And, counter to what might be expected, such an overview need not be immediately obsolete due to the fluid details of technology: if guidance for composition teachers can stay focused on how emergent technology shapes writing practices and environments, rather than on the nuances of the technology itself, a great deal of information can be summarized in some useful ways. Examining the ways in which CBPP affects writing environments and writers' motivations for composing will lead teachers of writing to the most concise and relevant key for translating rapid technological developments.

But it will take some work to make a useful connection between existing composition pedagogy and the future writing landscape of our students. Teachers of college writing *should* be confused, for the rhetorical foundation of their training, practices, research, and basic instincts as teachers has fragmented. Aristotle's touchstone rhetorical triangle—indelibly positioning us into the roles of speaker, speech, and audience—is less and less the monolith it seemed five years ago. Even contemporary appraisals, which accommodate the anxieties of postmodernist thinking, have been further ruptured by the continual evolution of computer applications that would appear to be furthest removed from the teaching of writing in the college classroom.

Wikis are a manifestation of CBPP and pose challenges for composition instruction. Wikis, like Internet chat, are virtually invisible within the majority of composition pedagogies. Our reluctance to identify, much less embrace, electronic writing developments lies in our training, our professional environments, and in our own experiences as writers. If composition training does not fully incorporate Internet writing environments such as wikis, however, then it will be difficult to spread awareness of the serious and sophisticated rhetorical acts performed in them. For our professional environments to value the original research of electronic environments and continue thoughtful inquiry into the rhetoric of Internet writing, writing teachers must observe, investigate, and research its use among our students.

As teachers and scholars, we will not develop a useful understanding of CBPP solely through a more sophisticated understanding of the technology that drives its devices. Even though an increased awareness of these technologies enhances our ability to understand the rhetorical boundaries of electronic writing, our appreciation of these new formats is not pinned to our comprehension of the underlying computer code. Rather, answers will come when we recognize that, as teachers of writing, we need to acknowledge the formats in which our students write, acknowledge writing that matters to them, and recognize the principles of critical thinking where they appear. To do this—to retrain our vision—we first need to look at how our rhetorical training can both bind and blind us.

The wiki is problematic for teachers of writing because it further dissolves those roles of writer, text, and audience that have been so thoroughly fragmented already by decades of postmodern theory. Yet, for this very reason, the wiki also is an exciting tool for student writers, for it is through the dissolution of rigidly defined roles of writer, text, and reader that students are becoming energized about writing. The immediacy of Internet chat allows participants to cycle through the roles of writer and reader, thereby accounting for some of that medium's popularity with student writers. Students who write in wikis cite some of these same reasons for an intense involvement with their text: they know that what they submit to a group collaboration document will be quickly—if not immediately—assessed and edited by other readers. At the same time, writers who are excited by the immediate feedback of readers are also challenged by another switch—that from the role of reader to writer—when the reader takes control of the text. This event—the crossing of role boundaries between reader and author—is such a fundamental aspect of the wiki writing environment that it becomes its dominant characteristic. In other words, wikis create an electronic group writing environment that permits collaboration on an entirely new level. Not only does this environment challenge the Aristotelian notion of the sole author, but it also challenges it with the massive network capabilities of the World Wide Web and its potential of incorporating writers from across the globe.

Therefore, we have several factors that help to account for composition pedagogy's failure to recognize fully and engage with the wiki as a relevant writing environment. An initial consideration is the fact that the wiki could still be labeled as an emergent electronic technology, even though it was first developed in 1995, and the academy has a history of lagging behind its students in adopting emergent electronic technologies. Additionally, the wiki challenges the sole-author paradigm, which creates resistance to its engagement on at least two more fronts. First, composition and rhetoric substantially fail to account for wikis; even though there is a significant, growing body of electronic rhetoric, it has yet to address how the wiki specifically and practically challenges composition pedagogy. While postmodern authors are adept at recognizing the fragmentation of the traditional classification of writer, text, and reader, there is room for additional pragmatic thought on how theories of postmodern or electronic rhetoric can inform the teaching of writing. The wiki is actually an example of a larger phenomenon—commons-based peer production—and CBPP presents a challenge to the stability of the rhetorical categories of author, text, and reader. Second, there is a gap in composition literature's explanation of wikis because they are clearly an example of collaborative learning, offering a new scale of collaboration not anticipated by much of contemporary composition theory. In the past, collaborative learning has entailed small writing groups—two to six individuals—within a larger group, such as a class. Wikis increase the number of collaborators easily to the thousands, and potentially to the millions.

Commons-Based Peer Production

CBPP was popularized by Yochai Benkler in "Coase's Penguin, or Linux and the Nature of the Firm" (2002). Benkler's title contains a double reference: Ronald Coase is the father of firm theory in modern economic thought, and the penguin is the official mascot of Linux, the most popular open-source operating system. Though Benkler is a law professor and his article was published in the *Yale Law Journal*, his analysis of human behavior within the phenomenon of open-source software is essentially grounded in economic theory. Benkler extends Coase's work, which offered a system for defining economic behaviors of individuals. Coase's philosophy can be very roughly summarized as follows: individuals will either work on their own or for someone else.

When we work on our own, we engage in what Coase calls the market model of production (Figure 1.1). Within the market model of production, individuals engage the market autonomously. The individual must independently determine what he or she can do to produce a product for the marketplace. The individual is responsible for interpreting the signals provided by the marketplace as to what it finds valuable; assessing all of his or her talents, capital, and collaborative potential; and then delivering a product to the market that is most advantageous for the individual. The signals sent to individuals as to what the market finds valuable are usually in the form of prices, and prices, though intermittent and variable, are final in their determination of the worth that a market places on potential products.

The alternative, according to Benkler, is the firm model of production (Figure 1.2). In the firm model of production, the individual reports not to the marketplace but to some form of management. The firm management inserts itself as a layer between the worker and the market, assuming many of the responsibilities formerly assumed by the individual in the market model: the manager interprets price signals to determine which of all the possible production combinations the firm could pursue and the market would find valuable. The manager also assesses the talents of workers to determine which products are within their capabilities, and the manager assesses resources (capital and information) for production. Additionally, the manager evaluates possible worker/resource combinations to find the most effective production route. On the other

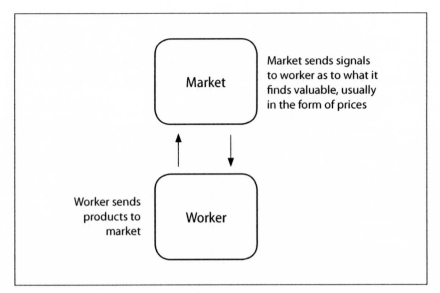

Figure 1.1: Coase's market model of production

hand, the worker surrenders the power of these choices to management in exchange for reduced risk. The worker no longer is allowed to decide what type of project is most suitable to his or her own talents, since management assumes the risks of interpreting market signals and delivering a worthy product to the marketplace.

Commons-based peer production, as defined by Benkler, represents an entirely new mode of economic production, distinguishing itself from both the market model of production and the firm model of production while retaining some aspects of both (Figure 1.3). CBPP is a recent phenomenon because it is a product of a pervasively networked environment, or in other words, the Internet. The rise of CBPP is strictly an information age event, as it is predicated on a marketplace model in a society where information is the key commodity. When the dominant economic factors are determined by costs associated with a traditional manufacturing economy, CBPP will not arise. According to Benkler, CBPP shines as a production model when four factors of an information age economy come into consideration. First, costs of fixation, or the costs to "fix ideas and human utterances in a media capable of storing and communicating them," must be low (377). Additionally, the costs of trans-

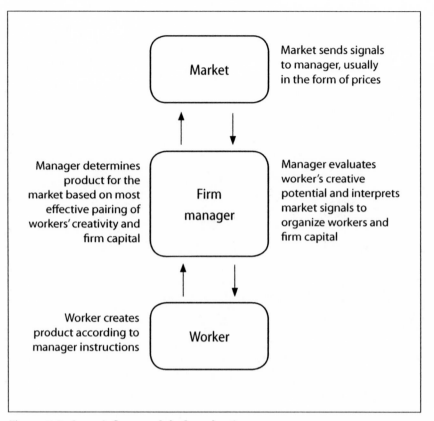

Figure 1.2: Coase's firm model of production

mitting ideas must be low. The third factor required for the emergence of effective CBPP is public information: CBPP only works well when all parties have access to the same information. If one party has proprietary or secret information or can otherwise act on information withheld from other participants, then the economics of CBPP fail. If these three factors are met, then the sole remaining scarce resource in production becomes human creativity. And CBPP is founded on the most efficient use of human creativity.

Benkler also states that CBPP models of production are marked by the following characteristics:

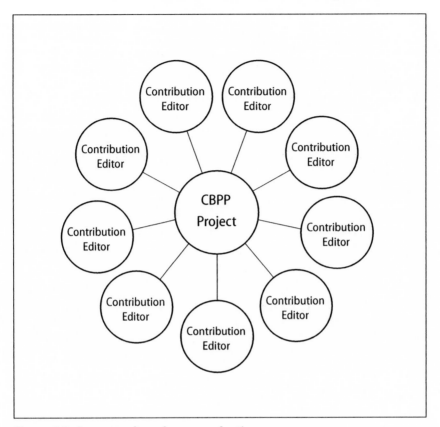

Figure 1.3: Commons-based peer production

- The work is modular. Work must be divisible into components that can be produced independently of each other, in any sequence. In this way people can work whenever it is most convenient for them, with whichever talents they have to offer, and with whomever they choose.
- The work is sufficiently granular. The size of the module must be small. If it is, people can work as much or as little as it interests them. This frees people to work without pay.
- The work has low cost integration. The project must be able to edit out weak or insufficient contributions. This must be done efficiently, at a low enough cost for the whole project such that the work does not fall to a small number of individuals.

One key similarity in all of these characteristics is that this model puts more choice and autonomy in the hands of individuals.

The thought of working for oneself, or with collaborators, is indeed an enticing prospect to anyone toiling away in an anonymous cubicle. It becomes easy to understand why CBPP excels at maximizing individual creativity, as it might produce the ideal workplace for nurturing invention: you work only on projects that interest you, only when you want to work, and only for as long as you remain engaged with the topic, and you collaborate with others who share that interest—but only when you want to. Yet there is still a marketplace that must be satisfied, often emphasizing the last, and most elusive, element of CBPP: low-cost integration. All CBPP networks must create an effective system of integration for contributions that is rigorous with, and encouraging of, its workers. Established CBPP networks Linux and Wikipedia have organic integration systems for their respective cultures. But in terms of establishing the systematic primacy of creativity, CBPP networks should be first appreciated for their ability to encourage individuals to self-identify their talents and possible contributions in light of a marketplace's desires. While the urgency of low-cost integration for a CBPP network is often emphasized, what is less appreciated is the fact that through its very structure a CBPP network makes the needs of the marketplace continually visible to its contributors, allowing them to self-edit their contributions even before submitting them to the CBPP network.

In CBPP, workers do not follow the price signals of a marketplace or the directions of a firm manager to determine their behaviors. Instead, workers act more as autonomous agents, or contributors, and select CBPP projects in which to participate based on their own internal motivations. Benkler writes that "peer production provides a framework within which individuals who have the best information available about their own fit for a task can self-identify for the task. This provides an information gain over firms and markets, but only if the system develops some mechanism to filter out mistaken judgments that agents make about themselves. This is why practically all successful peer production systems have a robust mechanism for peer review or statistical weeding out of contributions from agents who misjudge themselves" (2002, 375).

Though there is much more to say about CBPP, let us take a moment to consider how these economic models—Coase's individual, Coase's firm, and Benkler's CBPP—provide insight on the traditional model of teaching writing.

In the composition classroom, instructors primarily model the market writer, or someone who possesses enough writing acumen to communicate effectively in a professional environment. Within the academy, and especially within departments of English, we primarily value the "market" model of writing in our teaching. All of our traditional judgments about student writing, the traditional structure of our classes, and the end goal for our education of student writers have sought to develop writers' skills to the point of being able to engage an audience on their own, or, in Coase's terms, react with the market as individuals. This conception of the mature writer as being an individual sufficiently creative and properly trained to offer text with original insight for the professional audience is deeply imbricated with other romantic notions, but for the moment it will suffice to acknowledge that writing teachers train student writers with this goal of professional competence and autonomy in mind. The goal of college composition is to produce autonomous writers who engage the "real world" with proficient, readable, text that embodies a modicum of critical thinking.

As a market sends workers intermittent but important signals as to which products it finds valuable, so too do audiences send writers intermittent signals as to what they find valuable in the texts writers create (Figure 1.4). In the academic setting, scholars send writing for consideration to professional journals or book editors, and those individuals send return signals in the form of publication or rejection. Though the particular mechanisms for this communication may vary by field, the underlying mechanisms for acceptance or rejection are essential, consistent, and defining features of professional writing.

By contrast, instructors train students in a classroom according to the economic model of the firm: instructors play the role of the firm manager, coaching students up to the level of a market writer by standing in for that market, or ultimate audience, and judging student writing according to how they feel the market would judge it (Figure 1.5).

At the college level, the composition teacher claims the role of a successful market writer. He or she qualifies for teaching based on his or her track record of acceptable scholarly research in the form of publication, or, in Coase's terms, success in engaging the market independently,

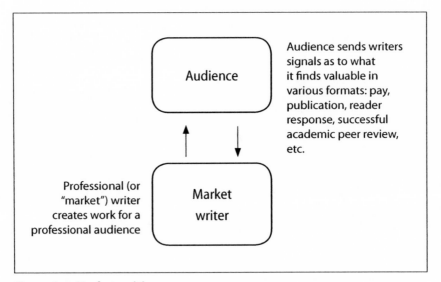

Figure 1.4: Market writing

and then trains his or her students to do the same. It is the composition teacher who both models Coase's market writer (he or she having successfully engaged the market/"real world" professional audience in building a track record of acceptable publications) and plays the role of firm manager (sending signals to the student writer on how to spend his or her time writing most productively until he or she is ready to take those signals directly from the marketplace/"real world" professional audience). Student writers do not compose for a professional audience; rather, they compose for a composition teacher who acts as a proxy for that professional audience, reflecting the attitudes and opinions of such an audience in his or her attempt to prepare the writers to meet the same. (As will be explored more throughout this book, it is exactly this very act of standing in for the professional audience that leads to much confusion and angst, as students invariably envision themselves as writing for the teacher, rather than some external audience, regardless of how thoroughly the teacher articulates another relationship.) If Coase's individual-to-market and firm-to-market models roughly parallel the institutionalized development of writers in the college composition format, then we can investigate how importing CBPP would affect traditional models of college composition.

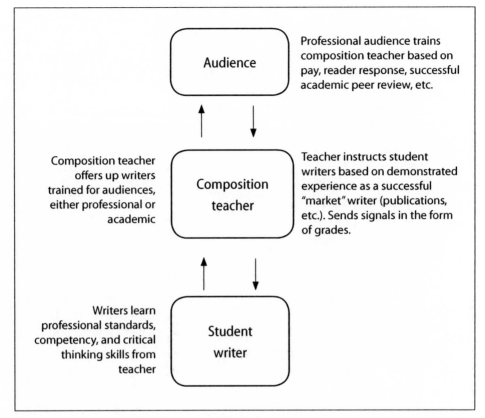

Figure 1.5: Firm model of the composition classroom

CBPP production differs from the market writer model and the classroom-as-firm model in several key aspects, but the unifying theme is that the CBPP model puts more control and responsibility into the hands of students, resituating the ancient rhetorical canon of invention. CBPP asks writers to select their own topics based on what the project or market finds valuable rather than allowing a writing teacher to select the topic. As will be further developed in Chapters 2 and 4, student writers in CBPP classrooms complain about many of the same problems that challenge professional writers—locating relevant and interesting projects that need their talents, developing expertise rapidly, negotiating feedback, and delivering only the most valuable information to readers. The tasks demand greater skill, training, confidence, flexibility, and support than those in the traditional classroom.

CBPP also sets a new standard for peer review. Without effective peer review, the CBPP model ceases to exist. Thus, this new classroom model requires that students engage in active peer review to decide which contributions are valuable to the overall writing enterprise and to justify tough edits. CBPP writing moves students closer to engaging an ultimate audience directly rather than working through the composition teacher as a proxy for some unspecified audience. Additionally, when students engage in successful peer review of others' contributions to the CBPP project, they must internalize for themselves the principles of effective composition. This internalization is brought to the foreground when student writers must defend their CBPP edits in terms of composition principles.

Perhaps least understood, and least examined, is the shift in ethos that accompanies incorporation of CBPP into the traditional composition classroom. Ultimately CBPP emphasizes the individual; by placing so many of the production decisions into the hands of individual students, CBPP fosters greater maturity and self-awareness. By breaking with a more hierarchical structure and replacing it with a networked structure, CBPP also better prepares students for the writing world they will engage after college. This unique structure allows CBPP to achieve a balance between individual and collaborative work. Educators who remain skeptical about collaborative learning have often decried the loss of the individual within team writing assignments; CBPP's emphasis on individual invention and collaborative peer review position a creative tension between these two extremes.

Finally, introducing CBPP into the composition classroom is a triumph for the identity of the individual and individual creativity. Economists praise CBPP systems for their ability to harness efficiently human creativity across a massively distributed network. This same emphasis on creativity, which is essential to the writing process, speaks of gains and human fulfillment beyond the lexicon of economics.

Economic Hesitations

Coase's most noted insight within the framework of firm theory is the existence of transaction costs for individuals. When individuals find that the transaction costs for working in a firm exceed what they would pay if working for the market alone, Coase theorizes that they would leave a firm to produce goods for the market directly.

Can the principles of CBPP further the goals of good writing instruction? In order to fully critique the proposition of importing CBPP to the composition classroom, one must give serious consideration to the underlying economic theory Benkler employs for explaining CBPP. Before going further, however, it is worth identifying from the outset some of the chief concerns readers might have for consulting economic theory to develop a more effective composition pedagogy. Even readers who might be willing to concede the aptness of economic theory for explaining the development of Internet writing systems such as Wikipedia can, and perhaps should, harbor concerns over the introduction of economic theory to explain systems for teaching writing. Primarily, composition is a pursuit located firmly in the humanities, and while economics is a discipline usually found in the business school, the fact remains that there are fundamentally different assumptions separating the two disciplines. Composition focuses on developing sound rhetorical principles to better define and promote good writing practices—a largely qualitative endeavor— while economics seeks to measure, understand, and predict human behaviors in response to material situations—a largely quantitative proposition. Juxtaposing these fundamentally distinct world views would seem to challenge the values of many composition and economic instructors; rather than provide a convincing model for revising composition strategies, importation of economic theory might well cost more in controversy than it offers in terms of solutions.

Consider a touchstone definition of economics offered by the early twentieth-century authority Lionel Robbins, who was known both for the breadth of his economic thinking and his opposition to Keynesian economics. Robbins offered that "economics is the science which studies human behavior as a relationship between ends and scarce means that have alternative uses" (1932, 16). As such, this definition offers a fruitful beginning point for recording objections for leaning on economics to clarify the structure and challenges of the electronic writing environment. First, Robbins categorizes economics as a science. While some in the sciences might object to the inclusion of economics among their fields of inquiry, economics insists on developing models to predict human behaviors and finding objectively verifiable measures to test those models. This insistence on quantification might well run counter to fundamental assumptions of contemporary composition pedagogy, which long ago diversified its theories and practices beyond the claims of a single, central, objective and verifiable truth that had become associated with current-traditional rhetoric. More simply put: writing is constructed as an inherently qualitative, not quantitative, pursuit. Additionally, economic theory as a tool for understanding composition pedagogy necessarily shifts the theoretical perspective towards material production, if not fully awakening the specters of materialism and Marxist literary theory. Fundamental economic concepts such as supply and demand emphasize aggregated human responses to material needs rather than the concerns of artful expression. Economics must, by its own self-definition, emphasize the measured over the immeasurable.

There also is great reluctance to look to economic theory as a basis for understanding humanistic pursuits in higher education, given the contemporary business-think climate of college administration, as documented in works such as Eric Gould's *The University in a Corporate Culture* (2003). From the 1990s onward, there has been an increasing tendency for higher education administrators to employ a business rationale for classroom decision making, which has seemed to many as the further abrogation of ethical responsibility to the invisible hand of the marketplace in yet another arena of public policy. Economics is a field that recently has moved to complicate some of its most basic assumptions—namely, that all individuals can be assumed to act out of a simple desire to improve their material situation—by adapting the advances of evolutionary biology and psychology (cf. Richard Dawkins's *The Selfish Gene* [1989] and Robert Frank's *Passions Within Reason* [1988]). Teaching to the baseline assumption that all students can, and must, act only toward fulfillment of their material best interests would run counter to liberal arts values and the fundamental assumptions of human development. Additionally, the economic model often summarizes the reality of complex human motivations by attempting to reduce them to a single, simple drive for material gain. Even if the economic model of human behavior is not counter to the ethics and aims of good teaching, to assume that students are motivated by nothing more than a consumer's desire for material gratification would obviate the more complex and ethically-developed relationship that sound pedagogy assumes, as well as naively reduce the cognitive reality of the learning process. Thus, we must be ready to interrogate the importation of economic theory into the writing classroom on the basis of its ethics and its oversimplification of the human condition, as well as its reconstitution of the student-teaching relationship into a consumer-producer model.

None of these objections, however, would seem to slow the recent advance of economic theory into areas previously regarded as out of bounds, illustrated by Steven D. Levitt and Stephen J. Dubner's *Freakonomics* (2005). To many contemporary observers, it would seem that the academy has already replaced much of the liberal arts culture that traditionally has hosted composition with a backdrop of business-speak and quantitative modeling. But the proper attitude to strike toward the importation of economic thought into the composition classroom ought to be held by the veracity of the model proposed. That is to say, if the model of electronic writing for the composition classroom is to be influenced by economic theory, then that theory should be judged by testing the outcomes predicted by the model. If CBPP can improve composition pedagogy, then we should challenge it to yield specific claims about improving student writing that can then be tested. This book will do just that, and it invites its readers to table any dis-ease about relying on quantitative assumptions of the economic disciplines until these specific claims for the benefit of composition pedagogy can be stated and tested.

Economic Analysis and Electronic Writing

Writing, as a discipline, grows more quantitative as it becomes more electronic. Sun Microsystems's corporate slogan captures this idea well: "The computer is the network." That is, the concept of computing is no longer primarily concerned with the processing capacity of the machine on the desktop or in a lab. Since the advent of the Internet, computing for most of us means connecting to a network and then making sense of those connections. Networked consciousness permeates writing, indeed, as it is no longer practical to theorize about writing without measuring the impact of the electronic environment. Networked consciousness has thus far been shaped as a download model, envisioning student writers as consuming information found on the Internet. The upload model, or "Web 2.0" concept, reverses the flow of information and transforms networking reality from consuming to contributing, a potential made most visible by Wikipedia. Writing is created, stored, and shared digitally, which means that it has become an inherently quantifiable affair. Student writers write from varying positions of awareness of these electronic dimensions and how they create an audience for their work, but the networked reality is nonetheless a permanent part of the writing landscape. Thus, contemporary composition itself bridges uneasily the gap between humanist pursuits and electronic realities—between the descriptive and the defined—and as such shares a concern with contemporary economics. Just as contemporary composition finds itself struggling to apply its own classical origins to a digital world, contemporary economics finds itself bending traditional quantitative concerns such as supply and demand to model infinitely more erratic human motivations and behaviors. The current and future concerns of both fields of knowledge are moving closer.

This unbounded nature of contemporary economics is marked by the field's official acceptance of work that once would have been considered either sloppy or simply non-academic. The best example of this phenomenon is the John Bates Clark Medal, given by the American Economics Association every other year to the most promising economist under the age of forty. The 2003 award was given to Steven D. Levitt of the University of Chicago. The choice is unconventional not only because of Levitt's stated dis-ease with the conventions of his discipline (he has been quoted as saying, "I just don't know very much about the field of economics. . . . I'm not very good at math, I don't know a lot about econometrics, and I also don't know how to do theory" [Levitt and Dubner 2005, x]), but also the fact that his focus is on matters considered beyond the traditional purview of economics. *New York Times* writer Stephen J. Dubner characterized Levitt's scope this way: "What interested Levitt were the stuff and riddles of everyday life. . . . As Levitt sees it, economics is a science with excellent tools for gaining answers, but a serious shortage of interesting questions" (xi). Levitt and Dubner thus collaborated on *Freakonomics*, a book that claims to map the analytical tools of economics onto completely new terrain—concerns beyond traditional production and consumption. For those who would seek to better understand how CBPP will reshape the composition classroom, the project of Levitt and Dubner is not so interesting either in terms of its veracity or its novelty. Salient instead is Levitt and Dubner's grounding of their work in a convincing definition of economics to justify for their readers why this particular field offers compelling insights beyond the imaginary widgets of so many econ classroom chalkboards. To do so, they wisely invoke Adam Smith in his original role as a moral philosopher—someone who studies what people ought to do—whose passion for accurate measurement of human behaviors led him instead to the inquiry of what humans actually do. They write, "It is worth remembering that Adam Smith, the founder of classical economics, was first and foremost a philosopher. He strove to be a moralist and, in so doing, became an economist. When he published *The Theory of Moral Sentiments* in 1759, modern capitalism was just getting under way. Smith was entranced by the sweeping changes wrought by this new force, but it wasn't only the numbers that interested him. It was the human effect, the fact that economic forces were vastly changing the way a person thought and behaved in a given situation" (14–15).

It is worth considering that we live in a similar time of behavioral revolution, where electronic networked writing is changing the way writers think and act. Just as Smith's pursuit of grasping and explaining new human behaviors led him across disciplinary boundaries in the eighteenth-century, so too does the attempt to understand the effect of wikis on writing necessitate a willingness to borrow tools from other disciplines to solve writing problems. Levitt and Dubner seem to anticipate this very dynamic when they write that "economics is above all a science of measurement. It comprises an extraordinarily powerful and flexible set of tools that can reliably assess a thicket of information to determine the effect of any one factor, or even the whole effect. . . . Since the science of economics is primarily a set of tools, as opposed to a subject matter, then no subject, however offbeat, need be beyond its reach" (13–14).

Robbins had offered his definition of economics in 1923. As Levitt's success in remapping economics would indicate, the field has greatly diversified since then and should no longer be understood as a monolithic enterprise. Managerial economics has emerged as a particular subfield that attempts to understand human behaviors and motivations outside the traditional problem set of classical economics. To be sure, managerial economics is concerned with business problems and business outcomes, but it positions itself on the border of human behavior and economic results, attempting to create principles for more effective management. While it retains many of the traditional aims and tools of traditional economics, managerial economics has also sought to apply the modeling and hypotheses developments of economic theory to the practical situations faced by business managers, who often encounter concerns that are not easily quantified. Managerial economics offers particularly valuable insights for the project of applying Benkler's CBPP theory to the writing classroom since it too is founded on firm theory. Thus, if we are to find a branch of economic inquiry that will help the project of applying economic thought to evaluate the composition classroom, managerial economics will provide that toolbox.

Nick Wilkinson, author of the textbook *Managerial Economics: A Problem Solving Approach* (2005), offers a definition for managerial economics that evokes Robbins's sense of economics as "choosing between scarce means that have alternative resources," but with a definite broadening of scope. He alludes to some of the possible readerly discomfort that has been expressed about the creep of economics from widgets to wikis:

> [Managerial economics is] the application of economic theory and methods to business decision making. . . . The term "business" must be defined very broadly in this context: it applies to any situation where there is a transaction between two or more parties. Of course, this widens the scope of the concept beyond the bounds that many people find comfortable: it includes taking someone on a date, playing a game with one's children in a park, going to confession in a church, asking a

friend to help out at work, agreeing to look after a colleague's cat while they are away, taking part in a neighbourhood watch scheme. In all cases, costs and benefits occur, however intangible, and a decision must be made between different courses of action. (8–9)

All writers are familiar with the terms of choosing between modes of expression to locate the best connection with an audience (what could better define rhetoric?), even if that connection is not the sole purpose of composition. The similarity here between communication and commerce lies within the rhetorical author's examination of all available expressions to make that strongest expression of an idea, just as within the material world an economic agent must consider all possible means of production before choosing a course of action. If electronic writing in the composition classroom can be viewed within the framework of a transaction, then the idea of employing economics to frame it becomes less of a controversial choice. The rhetorical triangle also prepares one to envision writing within the broader context of Wilkinson's managerial economic transaction: the writer, in preparing texts, considers the relative costs and benefits of particular textual choices—or their reception—before transmitting them to the reader. As Walter Ong has demonstrated in multiple essays on the topic, including "The Writer's Audience Is Always a Fiction" (1975), the writer must actively conjure the image of the audience. And just as the writer conjures the image of the audience, that same writer must do something for the reader to earn and maintain his or her attention. Yes, the writer must *transact* with the reader, and never more so than when the reader can register his or her reaction to the text within the immediacy of the electronic environment.

The writer/audience relationship serves as an organizational paradigm for relevant economic theories. Benkler asserts that the CBPP structure thrives because it reduces transaction costs; no manager is required to peer into the soul of a worker to identify and assess the range of her or his possible creativity and production. Coase identifies transaction costs as the key for the emergence of a firm. Wilkinson similarly identifies transaction costs as the first of six key economic factors that comprise of the economic theory of the firm. Thus, a look at transaction cost theory is needed.

Market Theory of Economics

"Market" is defined by Oxford's *Dictionary of Economics* as simply "a place or institution in which buyers and sellers of a good or asset meet." More aptly, however, the definition expands to include "in many cases the market is a network of dealers linked physically by telephone and computer networks" (Black 2002, 288). In contrast to defining the place, another economic dictionary focuses on the transactions that a market permits, defining them as "a collection of homogeneous transactions. A market is created whenever potential sellers of a good or service are brought into contact with potential buyers and a means of exchange is available" (Bannock, Baxter, and Davis 2003, 242).

The economic theory of the market is roughly equivalent to the theory of the rhetorical situation. In terms of its history, theory, and practice, comparing the development of the market to the historical, theoretical, and practical development of the rhetorical situation will inform an understanding of each concept. In fact, as is becoming increasingly clear through works such as Thomas L. Friedman's *The World Is Flat* (2006), the broad topics of capitalism, technology, and writing are best understood as developing in relation to one another rather than as separate entities. Capitalism serves as the trigger for technological development, and information technology acts as the tool that produces and defines text. While it is perhaps inviting to think of these connections in Marx's terms of base and superstructure, the importation of any particular theoretical school is not necessary to apprehend the basic historical outlines that allow the economic, technologic, and rhetorical connections.

In the abstract of "Coase's Penguin," Benkler summarizes efficiently the differences between market theory and firm theory by stating that "for decades our understanding of economic production has been that individuals order their productive activities in one of two ways: either as employees in firms, following the directions of managers, or as individuals in markets, following price signals" (2002, 369). Later, he adds that "people use markets when the gains from doing so, net of transaction costs, exceed the gains from doing the same thing in a managed firm, net of organization costs" (372).

But Benkler's description of CBPP jumps over any serious investigation of market theory. This is understandable; relatively few economic theorists are willing to address the topic directly. As it turns out, the relative invisibility of the concept of the market—an idea absolutely fundamental to any understanding of the workings of capitalism—is a measure of the saturation of capitalism throughout contemporary economic thought. Writing almost forty years ago, economic theorist John Hicks attempted a theoretical history of the concept of the market. In so doing, he addressed the problem of seeing the concept of the market as itself, and took as his starting point the concept that a rise of the market necessarily implies a pre-condition from which the market separates itself: "What was there before? . . . There was a stage in the development of economics . . . when economists were so wrapped up market economics they were unwilling to contemplate anything else—unwilling to grant that there was any other organization which could ever be a serious alternative" (1969, 9). Part of the reason why an economic historian would have difficulty finding theorists in his field who can even conceive of an economic condition prior to capitalism lies in the enveloping nature of capitalism itself: the dominant social paradigm does not necessarily invite questioning. On the other hand, the concept of the market is also inherently slippery, for it has two main components: the actual history of a cultural touchstone for buying and selling goods, or the marketplace; and the theory of the influence of that marketplace in our culture, or market theory. When we discuss the concept of the market as a driving, fundamental aspect of capitalism, we are more accurately discussing market theory, or the concept of how a potential, theoretical, and unrealized marketplace directs actual, practical, material decisions. But this theoretical market stems from a real historical market, or a place where people gathered to buy, sell, and barter goods found in almost every culture in every historical period. That marketplace, as opposed to market theory, is further categorized by (1) location, and (2) type of goods transacted in the marketplace.

Market Grammar

One starting place for understanding the concept of the marketplace— that ubiquitous cultural fixture wherein almost in all periods, people have gathered to buy or sell goods—is within a lengthy entry on "Markets" in *The Oxford Encyclopedia of Economic History*. Douglass C. North starts by noting that the type and nature of markets found in any given culture are an accurate statement of their moral, or religious, values: "Throughout history, people have held widely disparate views about the equity, efficiency, and morality of forms of exchange. . . . Religions usually have strong views about the morality of various markets, including usury and insurance, as well as the time and place of exchange, the use of a monetary unit, and broadly impersonal exchange. . . . A necessary condition for the development of markets was the evolution of beliefs justifying their equity, efficiency, and morality" (433). Once permitted, markets needed rules to ensure fair trade, and like all comprehensive systems, two sets of rules emerged: codified rules for equitable trade, as stated in written laws, and customary rules, as determined and practiced by cultural consensus. Both sets of rules need enforcement, which North subdivides according to which party of a theoretical trade conducts the actual rule enforcement: "Enforcement may be carried out by the first party, through self-enforcement; the second party, through retaliation; or the third party, through ostracism by other interested parties or coercive enforcement by private groups or the state" (433). Implicit in North's concept of "parties" are the basic agents in the market: a seller who meets a buyer with a commodity for sale. Before proceeding to look further into the development of the marketplace over time, it is worth returning to the idea given at the outset of this chapter, that the development of the market is similar to the development of the rhetorical situation.

The marketplace shares the basic outline of the rhetorical situation. The rhetorical situation is typically attributed to Aristotle, and although the exact origins of this concept are unclear, the basic triad of speaker/author, speech/text, and audience/reader remains relatively constant in descriptions of the rhetorical triangle. An initial comparison between the economic concept of marketplace and the rhetorical situation reveals three corresponding analogies: the marketplace seller can be equated to the rhetorical speaker, the marketplace buyer can be equated to the rhetorical audience, and the marketplace commodity can be equated to the rhetorical speech act. We can consider these roles equivalent by comparing the sale to the speech act. Consider that the sale in the marketplace acts as a rough approval of the buyer for the seller's commodity. This positions the speaker as seller, and audience as buyer. In the rhetorical situation, the audience either approves or rejects the speaker's speech. Certainly, many authors will be all too familiar with the idea of the audience's approval or rejection of their text, but in considering the sale of the commodity in the marketplace as an approximation of the audience's acceptance of speech, one can also consider the apparatuses that frame both sets of production: speech and commodity. Specifically, for the marketplace to function, both parties must agree on a framework of acceptable behaviors, and those behaviors must be expressed in terms of written rules and unwritten customs; likewise, in a successful rhetorical situation, the parties establish a framework of language rules, both formal and informal.

In this comparison between the rhetorical situation and market theory, the key substitution is speech or text for commodity. In terms of economics, the transfer of the commodity is expressed and analyzed in transaction theory. In terms of rhetoric, the transfer of the speech or text is also expressed and analyzed in transaction theory (cf. the discussion of James Berlin's work in Chapter 4). In economics, transaction theory focuses on the act between buyer and seller primarily to analyze costs of production, theorizing that either or both parties—buyer or seller—seek an arrangement that reduces transaction costs, allows for optimal access to trading partners, and maximizes profits or value. In the rhetorical situation, the speaker seeks a situation that allows for the most direct communication with the audience, both to maximize the comprehension of the utterance and to widen the audience. Thus, in seeking the optimal rhetorical situation, the speaker necessarily is looking for the lowest transaction costs—the ability to find the largest audience possible who can comprehend the speech with as little distortion and as much acceptance as possible. This correspondence—the comparison of economic theory's transaction costs to the rhetorical speaker's desire to be heard accurately—is singularly the most salient result in comparing the two theories. Economic theory has focused upon transaction theory to understand complex human behaviors in the arena of commerce; comparing economic transaction theory to rhetorical transaction theory invites a similar focus, perhaps with an increase in clarity from a new perspective. But transaction cost theory is the most important economic concept for interpreting the principles of CBPP in the composition classroom, as transaction cost savings are at the heart of Benkler's claims for greater communication, productivity, and creative expression.

Equating economic transaction theory with rhetorical transaction theory also implies an equivalence between the sale, or acceptance of the commodity from the seller by the buyer, with persuasion, or acceptance of the message of the speaker by the audience. There are some problems with this approach, and it is necessary to qualify this analogy of economy and rhetoric. First, the key difference between the two models rests on how much power we are willing to assign the audience or buyer. In the rhetorical situation, the audience can sample the text, accepting all of it, none of it, or a portion of it. Listening or reading does not necessarily imply acceptance or approval. In contrast, the marketplace model assumes that the buyer accepts or rejects the commodity in its entirety; in this case, audience approval is made manifest through a material object.

Yet, while the marketplace model might entertain a separation between the buyer's purchase of the commodity and the buyer's satisfaction with that same commodity, it typically collapses any such distinctions to the point of sale. It does not seek to address the mental states of either the buyer or the seller before or after the sale, insisting upon the commodity at the location of the market and at the time of the market as the ultimate expression of the desires of both buyers and sellers. This economic transaction is more like the utterance of speech than the text of the written word, since the permanence of the written word invites a complexity of thought and reaction that can later be expanded upon. Thus, this reduction of all desires into the measurable commodity—a fundamental premise of economic analysis—remains the greatest limitation to employing economically inspired analysis in the realms of rhetoric.

Yet this focus upon the point of sale is the redeeming strength as well as a critical weakness of economic thought. By limiting the scope of analysis to this one consistent point, a great deal of human behavior can be quantified; the laws of supply and demand are premised upon the point of sale and have provided a cornerstone for quantifying aggregate human desires since the introduction of modern economic thought. Yet, no economic theorist would presume that predicting or measuring the population's desire to purchase tires or shirts and planning productive behaviors based on those assumptions would yield a summative statement of the human condition, just as no rhetorical theorist would assume that the sum of the speaker's or audience's intellect is captured by the relative measure of the persuasion in an utterance. Still, the reductive power and insight of economic thought hinges on this ability to equate a buyer's purchases with acceptance and approval. Critics of government by the invisible hand—or the surrendering of governmental power to the dictates of the marketplace—have fought the equation of commercial exchange with the public will for as long as there have been market economies. At any given point in time, critics of capitalism have decried the commodification of otherwise complex social issues in societies with market economies, yet the same critics have also conceded that it is much easier to measure currency paid for a particular product and to argue that it equates a buyer's sense of approval than to argue that the relative silence of data on a given topic equates to public will. If an economist records that the public paid two billion dollars in the last quarter for Voice over Internet Protocol (VoIP) services, he or she can make a forceful claim that people generally prefer this new form of telephone services to the old telephone network.

If transactional economics works to measure and predict productivity in the information age, then we should at least consider how transactional rhetoric can be a starting point for measuring and predicting productivity in the information age. Which brings us to the threshold of the converse problem for rhetorical studies: how can a speaker be certain that the audience has heard the speech? Or understood, agreed with, or been affected by that speech? Each major period of rhetorical theory has assigned audience reception a different weight. Certainly one of the great strengths of the classical model of rhetoric is the assumption of immediacy—the idea that an audience, unlike the receiver of the written text, can hear and respond to the spoken word. And as Jay David Bolter and other rhetoricians of the electronic era have theorized, the immediacy of the electronic network technology has reified author awareness of audience reception.

But the potential dissonance from comparing transactional economics (based on the reality of a marketplace) to transactional rhetoric (based in the reality of making meaning) raises some questions, including whether the marketplace model assigns too much influence to the role of the buyer to be considered an accurate substitution for textual creation. In other words, what does the marketplace model offer for situations where the speaker speaks without any consideration of an audience beyond himself or herself? A situation where the author writes primarily for his or her own benefit, with no indication of preparing a text for acceptance by an audience, does have a rough equivalence in the marketplace model. In economic theory, there are instances where sellers are not selling a commodity but rather preparing an object for their own edification—the commodity is not created with the intention of sale in the marketplace, even if it has a later life as a commodity. It is important to note, however, that art and texts prepared only for the benefit of the creator often follow the same rules of communication; that is, even though the object is created not as a commodity for sale, it is often readable. Having outlined the basic correspondence between the market and the rhetorical situation, the next step is to focus upon modularization and communication.

Modularization and Commodification

Capitalism's division of labor and its modularization of tasks prefigures one of the most difficult challenges of writing in a CBPP environment—integrating contributions—and places that challenge in the greater context of overall economic trends.

CBPP's insistence on modularization is not new. In fact, modularization is almost five centuries old, because it is merely the latest extension of capitalism. But often the most polarizing aspect of CBPP is specifically its use in writing: the objection arises that writing, especially original prose, resists modularization. In writing about open-source projects, Steven Weber specifically mentions writing as a task that—like the construction of a cathedral, but unlike the construction of software—cannot be accomplished by multiple authors or with content distributed over a network: "You can diagram the syntax of a poem or write an essay about an underlying theme. To represent it all at once—and to do so in a way that communicates effectively to an outside observer—is a problem of a different order of magnitude, perhaps insoluble. That is why great poetry is almost always the product of a single creative mind" (2004, 58). Thus, Weber joins others in insisting that writing is a unique art that is somehow beyond the capabilities of collaboration. Thousands of programmers might be able to author a computer program or an encyclopedia article, but this argument insists that quality writing demands a type of integrative oversight that simply resists a division of labor.

Economics is a field that has given a great deal of thought to division of labor. Traditionally, its analysis is algorithmic or algebraic, assuming that all tasks can be subdivided into smaller components for completion and then reassembled. In practice, the complexity of reassembling subdivided work into a meaningful whole again is tragically underestimated. And yet this breakdown and reassembly is a necessary and quotidian aspect of capitalism. Thus Heilbroner and Thurow are unusually sensitive economists (writing collaboratively, it must be observed) when they note the particularly human impact of capitalism's division of labor, in which "the self-sufficiency of individuals was greatly curtailed . . . as work became more and more finely divided, the products of work became ever smaller pieces of the total jigsaw puzzle. Individuals did not spin or weave cloth, but manipulated levers and fed the machinery that did the actual spinning or weaving. . . . No one of these jobs, performed by itself, would have sustained its performer for a single day; and no one of these products could have been exchanged for another product except through the complicated market network. Technology freed men and women from much material want, but it bound them to the workings of the market mechanism" (1998, 22–23).

The implications of this continual subdivision of labor for the well-being of workers are simple enough to trace when the developments are material and historical; material wealth is always measured and then recorded. But does the history of capitalism and the Industrial Revolution accurately predict the future concerns for writers in CBPP environments? What happens to the individual author's manifestation of self when his or her work is originated and dispersed over a network?

Thus far, in comparing the rhetorical situation to the development of the market system, we have begun to think of how the roles of seller, commodity, and buyer are similar to the rhetorical roles of speaker, speech, and audience. Additionally, the change from the market, or the physical place where individuals trade, to market theory, or the arrival of capitalism and the industrial revolution, has started us on the path of considering the parallels between the modularization of material production through the Industrial Revolution and the modularization of text in the information age. If economics is the science of measuring and predicting material output in the industrial age, electronic rhetoric can become the science of predicting and measuring productivity in the information age. Or, to adopt Richard Lanham's terminology, we move from "an economy of stuff" to one of information, where directing the attention of information consumers becomes the scarcest resource: "In an economy of stuff, the disciplines that govern extracting material from the earth's crust and making stuff out of it naturally stand at the center: the physical sciences, engineering, and economics as usually written. The arts and letters, however, vital we all agree them to be, are peripheral. But in an attention economy, the two change places. The arts and letters now stand at the center. They are the disciplines that study how attention is allocated, how cultural capital is created and traded" (2006, xii). Lanham's perspective jumps forward to anticipate a revival of arts and letters based on its value of capturing the audience's attention. But before one can join him in appreciating a new role for the economics of the information age based on electronic rhetoric, a further look at the fundamental changes that permit such a transition is required, as well as an explanation of the profound shift in thinking that accompanied the transition from market to market theory. In truth, that transition is best explained by considering a similar shift in rhetorical theory, or the shift from spoken to written communication.

Marketplace to Market Economy, or Preliterate to Literate

The rhetorical situation's transition from the spoken to the printed word is in many ways similar to the transition of economic systems from feudalism to capitalism. In writing about this change from a preliterate to an alphabetic society, Eric Havelock notes the fundamental changes to literacy and culture that further strengthen the comparison to the shift of marketplace economic system from precapitalist times to capitalism.

Havelock sets the date of the transition from oral to written culture, at least in Greece, at about 700 BCE (1982, 15), but notes that it was certainly a gradual transition, and that there is a great deal of uncertainty about setting an exact date. But there is no uncertainty in the claims that Havelock puts forth in considering the impact of the cultural shift. Havelock's central claim is that the technological change of using alphabetic characters allowed a change in cognition, enabling a completely new level of complexity in thought. Havelock writes that "the change became the means of introducing a new state of mind—the alphabetic state of mind, if the expression be allowed" (7). Havelock seems to anticipate his own audience's objections when he continues to muse, "How such a change could or might come about is best understood by appreciation of a physical fact: the alphabet converted the Greek spoken tongue into an artifact, thereby separating it from the speaker and making it into a 'language,' that is, an object available for inspection, reflection, analysis. . . . If it were possible to designate the new discourse by any one word, the appropriate word would be conceptual" (8).

How, then, does the transition from oral to the written dimension compare to the transition from market to market-based economy? How does a market-based economy become conceptual? These transitions—from markets within an economy to market economy, and from oral rhetoric to written rhetoric—are equivalent because they allow for a new level of abstraction, permitting the rhetorical speaker/author or economic earner/seller to achieve distance from both the act and object of creation. As Havelock notes, the alphabet allows the writer to preserve a thought and give it sustained attention over time through the act of writing it. The transformation, however, is allowed only through the act of recasting thought in the terms of abstract alphabetic signs. The economic agent who sells a good in a market economy experiences a similar abstraction. By taking the act of economic production away from the precapitalist context of the creator's daily consumption, and instead preparing articles to be resold to another, the capitalist act of creation entertains a new consumer, or audience, beyond the self. The vegetable, tool, or clothing is being prepared for consumption by another, rather than for the creator, and this awareness of the consumer/audience creates a distance and greater level of abstraction between the creator and the object, just as the act of writing allows the author to more readily distance himself from the thought than the preliterate speaker.

As Heilbroner and Thurow note, this aspect of the Industrial Revolution is famous for creating great alienation in the masses of workers who created soles, heels, laces, or uppers rather than shoes (23). It is equally famous for creating great wealth: the accompanying transition allowed an increase of productivity through an increase of efficiency. Marx would point out that this transition of productivity accumulates wealth only for those who owned the means of production, while defenders of capitalism would argue that the increased productivity meant that the workers are also consumers, enjoying the benefits of a material culture. What should also be noted, however, is that the transformation also created permanence by establishing an ideal type in the mind of the worker. Rather than creating a shoe for personal gratification, the market economy Industrial Revolution worker participates in assembling a shoe according to an ideal type—presumably one that would be purchased by an idealized consumer. The worker need not have a managerial position or participate in the shoe assembly to anticipate the ideal type; he or she can still produce a sub-part according to the ideal type. The important aspect of this shift is that, under the capitalist model of production, there must be communication about producing a concrete product based upon an abstraction. This communication or coordination is a production cost in firm theory, as will be shown later, but anticipates the challenges of textual content integration within CBPP: workers on the line must communicate with managers about the assembly of their components into shoes, paving the way for the CBPP conversation about how low-cost content integration among multiple writers creates a readable Wikipedia article. All output needs to be coordinated to create a shoe that will be purchased in the marketplace.

In spoken rhetoric, the immediacy of the audience means that the creation of the message never moves too far beyond audience approval. Like the precapitalist worker who makes the shoe for his or her own benefit and satisfaction, in the rhetorical situation the audience and consumer are never far from the creation process. Even if the precapitalist worker creates the object to sell to another person, the consumer is most likely someone the worker has a relationship with—either as a family member or through his or her professional reputation in a local market. In either case, that consumer is much more connected to the creator, mentally dominating the creative process, with the object of creation being closely associated with the creator's person. Similarly, the audience of the spoken word dominates its reception to the point of influencing its creation. The audience of the spoken word almost always has the ability to speak back to the creator of the speech. Even if the circumstances of the speech greatly inhibit the audience from speaking (e.g., at a reverent ceremony, or in a crowded theater, or in a paid town hall meeting), merely the fact that the audience can speak can create a deterrent for the speaker. Thus, the transition from spoken to written word and from precapitalist to market economies represents a new distance between creator and receiver, as well as a new level of permanence and abstraction.

This transition toward greater abstraction—either in the marketplace to market theory transition or the spoken rhetoric to written rhetoric transition—is crucial to anticipating the objections to and difficulties of understanding writing in the networked environment or CBPP. CBPP or networked writing combines the immediacy of spoken rhetoric with the increased abstraction of the written word; this much has been observed in the transition from letters to e-mail. CBPP writing can introduce a greater degree of anxiety about audience for the writer, not only because the audience can respond to the author's writing with the speed of oral culture, but also because the audience can collaborate in the written product. Thus, each stage represents a new level of anxiety: the precapitalist shoemaker knows well the wearer of the shoe, the industrial shoemaker makes shoe parts later assembled for a stranger, and the information age producer cannot even separate the role of creation and consumption, since the receiver can at any time become the creator. This overall problem of fragmentation and destruction of the creative context is specifically forecasted in the work of Karl Marx.

Marx's Commodity Fetishism Predicts the Problems of Modularization

In *Capital* (1867), Marx introduces the key concept of commodity fetishism. Commodity fetishism, however, is premised upon two of Marx's earlier economic definitions, "use value" and "exchange value," which are part of the larger concept of Marx's theory of labor value. For Marx, each material item possesses a baseline use value, or utility: "The utility of a thing makes it a use value. But this utility is not a thing of air. Being limited by the physical properties of the commodity, it has no existence apart from that commodity. A commodity, such as iron, corn, or a diamond, is therefore, so far as it is a material thing, a use value, something useful" (1996, 46).

The accompanying concept to use value is exchange value. Exchange value is simply what one commodity is worth in trade for another. For any given commodity, there is a variable exchange value in relation to another commodity—e.g., so many bushels of corn will bring so many quarts of oil. As a further distinction, Marx commentator Edward Reiss notes, "Exchange value and use value are not necessarily related. Air, for example, has a great use value, but zero exchange value" (1997, 97).

But Marx does trace one particular aspect of exchange value back to each produced commodity: labor. For Marx, the ultimate value within the commodity lies within the fact that human labor has created it. To assert this connection to labor, Marx writes that "it is only by being exchanged that the products of labour acquire, as values, one uniform social status, distinct from their varied forms of existence as objects of utility" (1996, 84). Once one loses sight of the fact that all value in the commodity is created only through human labor, the path is set for commodity fetishism.

Commodity fetishism is the unique transformation upon which much of modern economics, at least in Marx's view, is predicated. Exchanging the commodity opens the door to fetishizing it because it fools us into believing that the value of the commodity is somehow inherent in that object, rather than the result of the human labor required to create it. One paragraph in particular from *Capital* explains this concept most directly:

> A commodity is therefore a mysterious thing, simply because in it
> the social character of men's labour appears to them as an objective
> character stamped upon the product of that labour; because the
> relation of the producers to the sum total of their own labour is
> presented to them as a social relation, existing not between themselves,
> but between the products of their labour. This is the reason why the
> products of labor become commodities, social things whose qualities
> are at the same time perceptible and imperceptible by the senses. . . .
> There is a physical relation between physical things. But it is different
> with commodities. There, the existence of things *qua* commodities,

and the value relation between the products of labour which stamps them as commodities, have absolutely no connection with their physical properties and with the material relations rising therefrom. There it is a definite social relation between men, that assumes, in their eyes, the fantastic form of a relation between things. . . . This I call the Fetishism which attaches itself to the products of labour, so soon as they are produced as commodities, and which is therefore inseparable from the production of commodities. (1996, 82–83)

Fetishism, then, is the mistaken belief that value rests in the object itself rather than in the human labor that created the commodity. This condition is enabled through the decontextualization of the commodity from the conditions of its production into a new level of abstraction via exchange value. And exchange value is necessarily created through the act of selling (or, strictly speaking, trading) the object at the market. Thus, the market serves ostensibly as the vehicle to permit exchange value, but in reality also enables commodity fetishism.

Of course, many reject Marx's economic theory. In fact, most classical economists reject the notion of the labor theory of value outright, insisting instead that the market mechanisms of supply and demand determine the true value of commodities. Regardless of one's position on labor theory, Marx's complaint that commodity fetishism allows one to misconstrue the true value of the commodity because it has lost its relationship to human labor is similar to the problem of how modularization allows distortion of the value of writing in CBPP, raising the stakes for Benkler's low-cost integration to reassemble information in a meaningful way. In CBPP, it is vital that the multitudinous contributions to a project be assessed for accuracy and relevance, two qualities stripped from them upon their separation from the act of composition. What remains to be seen is whether CBPP possesses the power to render the same pervasive cultural transformation within the context of information technology that commodity fetishism has wrought within capitalist culture—whether the commodification factor of rendering information in discreet bits will permit readers to build upon it an entire culture of desire and material gratification, similar to the way in which commodity fetishism has allowed consumerist culture to transform postmodern identity.

Within this context, it is possible to consider wikis as tools of information commodification, acting as information decontextualizing machines—grinding thoughts into atomic particles, transmitting them over wavelengths, and then reassembling them at later points, devoid of authorial and content context, to question whether or not wikis play the role of "information commodifiers" is testament to the durability and permanence of Marxian capitalist economic theory as it reaffirms itself in the information age. In commenting on the durability and ubiquitous nature of capitalism, Fredric Jameson employs a phrase that will strike readers as particularly apt to our discussion—"the rhetoric of the market" (263). Yet Jameson refers to market rhetoric in terms of the basic building blocks of the cultural language of capitalism. In *Postmodernism*, he writes, "This allows me to express my thesis in its strongest form, which is that the rhetoric of the market has been a fundamental and central component of this ideological struggle, this struggle for the legitimation or delegitimation of left discourse" (1990, 263). Our focus on the market, then, as a mechanism for apprehending the broad technological shifts that permit economic transformations, is further legitimated as the operating metaphor for the shifts in language and knowledge production. Jameson's use of the term "market rhetoric" is equated with the idea of capitalist rhetoric, but is also apt for Benkler's approach to CBPP as a new mode of economic production. At the outset of this chapter, we gestured to the fact that economists Heilbroner and Thurow saw technology as a historical part of economic development. This discussion invites us to think of electronic writing as connected to the historical development of economic forces as well, but Jameson's phrase "rhetoric of the market" can now be seen with a double meaning: not only does the dominant cultural paradigm control the terminology of discourse for its own legitimation, but it also predicts our investigation of the history of economics to find the future of rhetoric.

The most common concern for writing over electronic networks such as CBPP is that writing, unlike material goods, once modularized, becomes susceptible to the same process of commodity fetishization: once the text is taken out of its original context, it becomes more difficult to understand but easier to misappropriate. Text, so this argument would go, is similar to Marx's commodity in that it obtains its value from the context in which it is created and through proximity with the author. Like the commodity that is manufactured for resale rather than the good that is created for personal or familiar use, text that is detached from the author and removed from the context of the accompanying text through the electronic process of modularization not only demands what Benkler dubs "low-cost integration" in order to be reassembled with other texts to make meaning, but also perhaps loses permanently the ethereal quality of "soulfulness," or connection to the author. Again, it is Marx's concept of commodification—the stripping away of the sense of value based on human labor—that best predicts the outcome of text that undergoes the process of modularization.

1.0, 2.0, 3.0

To get some perspective on the market, firm, and CBPP models and to see them as equivalents of oral rhetoric, written rhetoric, and electronic rhetoric, it is useful to return to Thomas Friedman. In his wide-ranging translation of current issues known as *The World Is Flat*, Friedman offers a 1.0/2.0/3.0 classification scheme for understanding globalization, stating that

> there have been three great eras of globalization. The first lasted from 1492 . . . until around 1800. I would call this era Globalization 1.0. It shrank the world from a size large to a size medium. Globalization 1.0 was about countries and muscles. . . . The second great era, Globalization 2.0, lasted roughly from 1800 to 2000, interrupted by the Great Depression and World Wars I and II. This era shrank the world from a size medium to a size small. In Globalization 2.0, the key agent of change, the dynamic force driving global integration, was multinational companies . . . right around the year 2000 we entered a whole new era: Globalization 3.0. Globalization 3.0 is shrinking the world from a size small to a size tiny and flattening the playing field at the same time. And while the dynamic force in Globalization 1.0 was countries globalizing and the dynamic force in Globalization 2.0 was companies globalizing, the dynamic force in Globalization 3.0—the force that gives it its unique character—is the newfound power for individuals to collaborate and compete globally. (2006, 9–10)

Friedman's schematic is useful for this discussion, which is concerned less with the larger trends of globalization than with the specific role of CBPP as an extension of two earlier economic stages. So far we have worked on a different tripartite categorization scheme: 1.0 would pair oral rhetoric and precapitalist economics, 2.0 would pair written rhetoric and capitalist economics, and 3.0 would offer electronic rhetoric for commons-based peer production. Having mapped the implications and analogies of the market model, it is time to look in more detail at the firm model.

The Economic Model of Firm Production

What is a firm? Benkler identifies it as an organization that emerges when individuals choose to work for a manager (372). Alchian and Demsetz have labeled the firm as a nexus of contracts, meaning that the firm can be viewed as a part of a "hub-and-spoke system," classical economists having theorized that a firm has legal contracts with its suppliers, workers, and customers that define all of its business relationships, the sum total of which is the definition of a firm (1972, 24). A more comprehensive approach to firm theory is offered by Louis Putterman and Randall S. Kroszner in their introduction to *The Economic Nature of the Firm* (1996). They acknowledge first the work of Ronald Coase, which put forth the idea of the firm as a legitimate object for study when relatively few in the field were willing to envision it as such and offered the idea of transaction costs: "Coase initiated the contemporary literature by pointing out that when economic agents interact with one another, they incur 'transaction costs' that vary with the mode of interaction" (9–10).

Moving forward to contemporary managerial economics as explained by Nick Wilkinson, one sees more of a focus on transactional economics. Wilkinson begins with the observation that in certain pursuits, there are benefits to co-operation and specialization (2005, 24), and the logical starting point for understanding firms is to acknowledge that economic actors work together when there is a joint understanding of an improved material situation. Yet Wilkinson notes that, when individuals gather to create a business enterprise—whether it is a corporation, partnership, or sole proprietorship—the firm is primarily a "legal fiction which simplifies business transactions because it enables the firm to contract bilater-

ally with suppliers, distributors, workers, managers, investors, and customers, rather than there being a situation where each party has to enter
into complicated multilateral arrangements" (22). Further, much of the
economic theory that predicts what type of preconditions will give rise to
particular economic organizations centers around the concept of transaction. Indeed, the transaction between two parties, whether they are individuals or firms, becomes the cellular level of economic organization. As
has been mentioned above, transaction cost theory becomes the key for
justifying the existence of the firm. Wilkinson offers that there are five
main areas of economic theory at play in defining the nature of the firm:
information theory, motivation theory, agency theory, property rights
theory, and game theory (22).

For the purposes of mapping out the composition classroom in the
electronic environment, it is necessary to examine only transaction cost
theory, motivation theory, and property rights theory. Wilkinson notes
that transaction cost theory is broken into two sub-components: co-
ordination costs and motivation costs. Co-ordination costs include search
costs, bargaining costs, and contracting costs. Search costs involve what a
buyer and seller must pay in order find another party to the transaction.
Bargaining costs address the amount of time either a buyer or seller pays
in order to reach an agreement on price, and contracting costs are associated with formalizing the terms of the transaction. Motivation costs, on
the other hand, are further broken down into the categories of hidden
information and hidden action. Hidden information addresses the situation of information asymmetry, or the condition where one party in the
transaction has an informational advantage over another (e.g., the seller
of a used car presumably knows more about the car's true condition than
the buyer; the buyer of a new car who has completed a great deal of Internet research might actually know more about what a new car is worth
than does the seller). Hidden action refers to the cost of keeping parties
honest; most economic scenarios assume that the parties "do what they
say and say what they mean," but in reality almost everyone has paid a
price for dealing with a deceptive buyer or seller (22–32).

Wilkinson notes further that one of the main conclusions of transaction cost theory as it relates to firm theory is that there is an assumed
point of transaction-cost-maximization for a firm: transacting with a
market is easier for an individual within the firm, as the firm pays for

the overhead of doing business, but as firms grow larger and that share of overhead increases for each individual, there will come a point when overhead costs are unsustainable.

CBPP, then, can be seen as a lowering of some firm costs. Motivation costs, or the identification of what person has the right skills for a particular project, are put up as the responsibility of the individual. This ability to self-assess is offered as the great insight of CBPP, since the individual can most accurately assess his or her own interests, and for what duration she or he will stay motivated to work with a project. What motivates people to work in a firm? Wilkinson notes that firms are composed of individuals, and that if a theory of a larger firm is to make any sense, it must first make sense on the individual level. This juncture also represents the weakest abstraction and grossest oversimplification of economic thinking: theorizing that an individual acts purely out of material self-interest. While successful contemporary economic theory no longer operates on such complete reductions, it does at least begin with the baseline assumption that people will reliably act in terms of their self-interest, most of the time. Exceptions that trouble economic models founded on self-interest include altruism, or as Wilkinson defines it, "any behaviour which confers a benefit to others, while involving a cost to the originator of the behaviour, with no corresponding mutual benefit" (27). Equally troubling is the converse, spiteful behavior, which Wilkinson defines as imposing "a cost upon others, while also involving a cost to the originator of the behaviour, with no corresponding material benefit" (27).

Thus, the engine that drives most every economic model—the "man on the street" who acts only out of self-interest—is fundamentally limited not only by the fact that self-interest fails to account realistically for the complex emotional, psychological, and moral drives that determine our behaviors, but also for the fact that even the self-interest abstraction contains the important caveats of altruism and vandalism. Given these limitations, should we not then be prepared to abandon economic modeling as fundamentally flawed and hopelessly inaccurate? Benkler writes of the difficulty in applying market mentality to account for the larger social effect of an information network:

> If there is one lesson we can learn from globalization and the ever-increasing reach of the market, it is that the logic of the market exerts

enormous pressure on existing social structures. If we are indeed seeing the emergence of a substantial component of nonmarket production at the very core of our economic engine—the production and exchange of information, and through it of information-based goods, tools, services, and capabilities—then this change suggests a genuine limit on the extent of the market. Such a limit, growing from within the very market that it limits, in its most advanced loci, would represent a genuine shift in direction for what appeared to be the ever-increasing global reach of the market economy and society in the past half century. (2006, 18–19)

Whether or not markets themselves begin to account for human motivations and network behaviors, the CBPP model of economic production further challenges the counter-assumptions of altruism and vandalism. Both of these concepts are important in understanding why wikis work. Altruism is a phenomenon that can account for some of the complex human motivations yielding the tremendous growth of Wikipedia: what happens when you lower the cost of altruism so that one party in a transaction can share knowledge with little or no expense? (Think of how one responds when occasionally asked directions by a stranger on the street—the vast majority of people are willing to help out when it costs them little, and they receive the benefit of feeling like experts.) The term "vandalism" is also a well-known concept for wikis, referring to an incident where one contributor erases another's contributions without justification. Both altruism and vandalism will play important roles in our descriptions and modeling of knowledge growth in wikis, and they are both forecasted herein as essential to understanding the economic theory of the firm.

The last area of firm theory necessary to this discussion is property rights theory. Wilkinson identifies property rights theory as important to understanding how the firm operates in that it defines what rights both parties might have towards commodities in a transaction even after the transaction has been completed (29). The two main issues are residual control and residual returns. Residual rights of control follow the asset out of the transaction; one might purchase a copy of a book, but is not free to make and sell unlimited copies of that text. Similarly, residual returns are the rights to revenue that follow the asset. In the

Table 1.1: Theoretical organization chart

Benkler	Rhetoric	Economics	Friedman
Market model	Oral rhetoric	Precapitalist market	1.0
Firm model	Written rhetoric	Capitalist/ market society	2.0
Commons-based peer production	Electronic rhetoric	Information age	3.0

above example, royalties from the sale of the book or its further reprinting would be residual returns.

Having attempted to trace the origins of CBPP across—in some cases—thousands of years, it might be helpful to offer a rough guide for keeping the multiple authors and theories in place (Table 1.1).

This chapter has attempted to identify many of the important trends and connections among these modes of thought, in order to prepare the reader to predict the value of CBPP for the teaching of writing in the academy and understand its potential as well as its limitations. With this understanding of the theoretical origins of CBPP, it is now time to see it in practice in the writing classroom.

2

A Wikipedia Writing Assignment for the Composition Classroom

What would a composition teacher who has never used a wiki and wants to try it need to know? The purpose of this chapter is to answer that question by providing a practical plan for incorporating wiki writing into the composition classroom. For teachers at the college level whose practice lies beyond the composition classroom, the last section of this chapter will specifically address the concerns of involving wiki writing in other areas of curriculum. As this plan for integrating wiki writing in the classroom progresses, it will explicitly connect back to the principles of good composition practices as enumerated by the Conference on College Composition and Communication (of the National Council of Teachers of English), as well as the Council of Writing Program Administrators (WPA). This plan of action will expand on those accepted composition principles by combining them with the concepts enumerated earlier, including

- **Laziness**, or maximizing student autonomy (and thus capability) by allowing them to select projects or topics based on their interests;
- **CBPP**, or maximizing the value added to collaborative projects through individual creativity and allowing the writing teacher to assume the role of writing "coach";
- **Authenticity**, which seeks to involve students in projects with audiences beyond the academic classroom;

- **Professional Standards**, by asking students to produce work both relevant to the overall project and credible in terms of ethos, with a reasoned voice and a sense of the values of that knowledge community;
- **Epistemology**, by asking students to understand the accepted knowledge-making procedures for their project's community, and, if necessary, to reevaluate or defend their contributions, when challenged, by the stated acceptable practices of that knowledge community;
- **Transition**, or moving the student from a position of being a consumer of general knowledge to the position of being a producer of specific, authoritative knowledge.

Sample Wiki Writing Assignment

The starting point for any teacher begins with the writing assignment, or course unit.

The following is a sample wiki writing assignment for a first-year composition (FYC) class. Examining how this one assignment is constructed will reveal the underlying options a teacher must consider in creating a wiki writing assignment. The assignment below is based on one used in my FYC course at the University of Georgia (UGA) in 2005, but it has been improved slightly based on lessons learned during that semester and beyond. This particular course was the second semester in the FYC sequence, and as on many college campuses, English 1102 at UGA focuses on applying the skills of critical thinking to the field of literature. In my course, I included a unit on film. "Assignment 4," then, is a wiki writing assignment that asks students to contribute to Wikipedia's film pages.

Assignment 4: Writing About Film in Public Spaces
Assignment Steps

For this last out of class project, we will contribute to film pages for Wikipedia, the online encyclopedia. Here are the major tasks of this project, presented in the order in which they will be tackled:

1. The first aspect of the project will be to identify, review, and assess Wikipedia's goals and policies to determine how our information can best contribute to the goals of that larger project.
2. The second task will be to decide which film you will write about, and whether you will work with a group or on your own.
3. The third task will be to examine Wikipedia film pages to determine the rhetorical elements of the best pages. How would you determine the best pages? You can look at longer pages, most revised pages, most visited pages, etc., but it is best to survey pages that are well-developed, and then identify common elements of style. Once you have a feel for what makes a good Wikipedia film page, you can then assess the film page topic of your choosing.* You will need to describe what you think can and should be improved.
4. Propose your project to the class in a brief (5–7 minute), informal presentation. Explain to us your topic, what you want to change, and why those changes will both improve that Wikipedia page and further the development of your own writing skills. Stronger presentations will reference both the "five pillars" of Wikipedia and our course outcomes.
5. Make your changes to the page. Write out the changes in advance on a word processor. Be sure to register with Wikipedia, and log in each time you access the site. Also, send me your login name. Before you save edits, make sure to use the preview function to read through the proposed changes, and explain your changes in the edit summary box.
6. Once you have begun making your contributions to the page, be sure to document on the discussion pages what you are changing and why you think those changes improve the page in terms of Wikipedia's own style. N.B. There is a high probability that what you write will be changed by another person on Wikipedia. Don't get upset.

---

* Some Wikipedia knowledge communities, including film, have organized themselves as WikiProjects to articulate best practices and nominate pages for internal peer review. The film project has created its own style guideline. Thus, if your writing assignment covers a Wikipedia topic that has formally organized itself as a project, you should consult their project page to help you articulate the appropriate headings on pages, though you need not feel compelled to accept the project's views as final. For more about projects, see *http://en.wikipedia.org/wiki/Wikipedia:WikiProject*.

7. Compose a reflective essay that assesses this writing experience and the development of your writing skills.

Overall, your mission here is similar to an informative essay that seeks to explain a concept to the reader. Since you are contributing to an encyclopedia project, you will not contribute "original research" or argue a thesis on a topic. Rather, your mission is to attempt to summarize the state of knowledge on the given topic and convey an ethos of expertise on the subject.

Assignment Calendar

Session 1: Monday

Project Overview. Read and review assignment.
Wikipedia Orientation: Review the "five pillars" of Wikipedia at
    http://en.wikipedia.org/wiki/Wikipedia:Five_pillars.
Skim through film pages.
Ponder your group or solo status.

Session 2: Wednesday

Before today's class, compose 250 words or more on the following: Write out a description of your understanding of Wikipedia, its goals, its problems, and how you feel contributing to the site will or will not help your writing skills. Upload it to our electronic course management site (<emma>) as Assignment 4, Stage 1.

In class today, determine whether you are going to work alone on a film page or work with others. (If you work with others, you will all receive the same grade. No groups larger than four, please.)

Also in class today, determine which film page you will work with. If there is a WikiProject page for your topic, consult it to see if pages have been listed as needing improvement or creation. See a list of WikiProject pages at http://en.wikipedia.org/wiki/Wikipedia:WikiProject .

Session 3: Friday

Before today's class, compose 250 words or more on the following: Complete a rhetorical analysis of Wikipedia film pages. Examine at least eight film pages. Read them and identify their common rhetorical elements. What makes for an adequate film page in Wikipedia? What makes for a better film page in Wikipedia? Be sure to consult the Wiki Project page for film, *http://en.wikipedia.org/wiki/Wikipedia:WikiProject_Films*. Upload it to our electronic course management site (<emma>) as Assignment 4, Stage 2.

In class today, chalkboard what we found and try to reach consensus on which elements we feel a page must have to be considered complete (essential elements), and then identify the elements that we feel define the best film pages (best practices). I will post our conclusions on our electronic course management site (<emma>).

Session 4: Monday

Before today's class, compose 250 words or more on the following: Identify the film page you are working on. Using your description of the elements of a good film page from the last assignment, what changes do you think your film page needs? Explain your topic, what you want to change on the Wikipedia page, and why those changes will both improve that Wikipedia page and further the development of your own writing skills. Stronger drafts will reference both the five pillars of Wikipedia and our course outcomes. Be sure to create your Wikipedia login and include it at the end of this text so that I too can find your contributions on Wikipedia. Upload it to our electronic course management site (<emma>) as Assignment 4, Stage 3.

In class today, give a brief (5–7 minute), informal report. Explain your topic to the class, what you want to change on the Wikipedia page, and why those changes will both improve that Wikipedia page and further the development of your own writing skills. Stronger presentations will reference both the five pillars of Wikipedia and our course outcomes.

Session 5: Wednesday

Before today's class, compose 250 words or more on the following: Write out the actual edits you will make for your page. Identify the page and the changes you will make for each subheading (include subheads you will add to the page). Include a link to the page and talk page before and after you have made your changes—four links in all. Upload it to our electronic course management site (<emma>) as Assignment 4, Stage 4.

In class today, make those edits. We will handle Q & A for problems during class.

Session 6: Friday

Before today's class, monitor your pages. *Refrain from making changes and/or responding to any reactions in the discussion pages.* Instead, compose 250 words or more on the following: Reflect on the changes you have made to the page, and why or why not you feel they have improved the project. Do your contributions contribute to the value of the project by adding credible facts within existing categories, utilizing Neutral POV? Do your contributions integrate themselves with existing content on page, reflecting an awareness of what comes before and after? Does your prose reflect a professional and credible ethos? Does your writing reflect an awareness of the knowledge in the field? Are your contributions are well-researched, and do you provide credible documentation? Were your contributions acknowledged by other contributors? Upload it to our electronic course management site (<emma>) as Assignment 4, Stage 5.

In class today, discuss changes others have made to your pages and the appropriate response to those changes. If others have removed your text, you should open a dialogue with them as to why they have done this, and then, after considering their responses, revise your text and repost it. If you get no response, then consider whether your text contributes to overall goals of Wikipedia (in reference to the five pillars and/or the WikiProject for your topic). If you choose to repost, cite those reasons in the discussion pages as your rationale for reposting. After today's session you are free to make changes you feel are necessary and/or desirable on the basis that they support the overall mission of Wikipedia.

Session 7: Monday

Before today's class, compose a 750–1,000 word reflective essay that addresses the following question: Has writing for a Wikipedia project developed your writing skills? If so, cite specific evidence from your contributions to Wikipedia. Where possible, interpret how those contributions have helped to develop your writing skills, either as defined by you and/or as defined in the course outcomes listed on the syllabus. Be sure to reflect not only on the text but also on the drafting process and your interaction with others in the class and on Wikipedia. If you do not feel that writing for Wikipedia has helped you to develop writing skills, then develop those thoughts as well. Look again at the course outcomes as well as your own expectations about what writing skills a course should develop.

In all likelihood, you will have evidence to support the claim that this assignment helped you to develop writing skills as well as evidence to challenge that idea. You need not feel bound to compose a paper that completely supports or challenges this experience and the development of your skills; rather, you should look for a holistic stance. Use MLA format. Upload it to our electronic course management site (<emma>) as Assignment 4, Stage 6.

In class today: Discuss changes others have made to your page, how you have responded, and how you plan to respond. Also, discuss your draft of the reflective essay. What challenges have you faced in composing it? What do you need to change before the next class session? (Optional: Complete peer review.)

Session 8: Wednesday

Before class today, complete the final draft of your reflective essay. Upload it to our electronic course management site (<emma>) as Assignment 4, Stage final.

In class today, continue observation of changes made to pages. Hold open discussion of which pages have had the most development.

What Does This Assignment Do for My Writers?

This assignment has four major stages for student writers: (1) orientation to Wikipedia as a CBPP host site, in terms of how knowledge is produced there and where the students can fit their contributions; (2) invention of content useful to that knowledge community, in keeping with the topic community's needs, the larger principles of Wikipedia (such as "neutral point of view"), and the standards of college composition; (3) negotiation of edits on Wikipedia, again within the standards of the Wikipedia project (including its code of conduct), within the topic community's values (reflecting a knowledge of film terms and measures), and the standards of college composition (respect for others' opinions but willingness to employ and receive critical thinking); and (4) reflection on the experience, with an understanding of the outcomes of a college composition course and willingness to self-assess. Each of these stages is expanded below to highlight their correlation to composition outcomes.

The first stage is spread out over Sessions 1, 2, and 3 in the assignment. In Session 1, you'll provide some information on the nature of Wikipedia and how your class will create content within that host. Here you will face a variety of challenges, not the least of which will be to allow students to simultaneously table and nurture their opinions on Wikipedia's viability as a resource while approaching it as a site for composition (more on that later). The orientation will continue in Session 2 as students evaluate content for their topic, film, with an eye toward where their thoughts might fit within the existing conversation. This session is fundamental to CBPP: here the writer is given maximum responsibility for selecting a topic, accurate to the demands of the discipline and relevant to the needs of the project, while also internally surveying his or her own creative preferences. Here the writer's creativity is balanced against the authentic needs of the professional project. The third session asks students to articulate their experiences as readers of the project's content, and then to apply the qualities of good writing from experience in the composition classroom. As students survey the film pages, they are being asked to develop and apply a sense of rhetorical purpose: Do these pages focus on a purpose? Do they reasonably meet the needs of multiple readers and respond to them with appropriate tone, voice, and formality? Do they integrate outside sources? Session 3 asks students to start examining which pages do these things well and to identify those elements which are essential to performing those functions.

The second stage, invention, occurs in Sessions 4 and 5 of the assignment. After your writers read and understand the existing content, they propose their additions. The class hears them out in an open discussion in Session 4. The students will have looked through at least eight Wikipedia film pages of their choosing, trying to discern the essential elements of what makes a good film page. They will combine that knowledge with their own personal preferences for working with a particular film, applying the "laziness" concept or marrying their own personal interests (subjective attraction toward a film project) with professional demands (producing text for a passing grade in your class). After they decide which page both interests them and would improve with their contributions, they must vet their project before the whole class. This procedure is an application of the CBPP model, in that the writing teacher—indeed the entire class—assumes the role of a coach rather than of an audience. With the teacher-as-grader distanced from the writer's field of view, the more legitimate audience—those who will actually read the Wikipedia film page—comes into view. Similarly, in Session 5, students compose and upload their texts. After the review of Session 4, the demands of a professional audience have been articulated more clearly. This process reinforces the accepted and encouraged composition practices of students employing multiple drafts, envisioning the writing process as open, understanding collaborative and social aspects of writing, learning to critique their own and others' works, and of course, using a variety of technologies to address a wide audience. Even more explicitly, the WPA outcomes under "Knowledge of Conventions" enumerates that students in composition courses should learn "to review work-in-progress in collaborative peer groups for purposes other than editing"; this second stage is tailored to support that outcome.

The third stage—negotiation of edits—takes place in Session 6. Students will find that their contributions to Wikipedia elicit a variety of responses: some text will be almost immediately erased without explanation; others contributions will remain on Wikipedia for years. In most cases, however, an average of these two extremes will apply. Most students will have had some text removed, and on the discussion pages there will be interaction with Wikipedia editors as to why they removed the text. In ideal Wikipedia practice, editors refrain from making changes and instead ask the contributors to change their submissions. In practice, this rarely happens. Most Wikipedians will remove your students' text without comment or with only a very brief comment. Instead of jumping into the fray, Session 6 asks your writers to reflect on their contributions: on whether or not they have improved the page, and why. If their contributions have been altered, students are asked to compose appropriate responses. All changes should improve the Wikipedia page in keeping with Wikipedia's mission as encyclopedia, and if students with removed text feel that it should remain, Session 6 will allow them space to practice those mission-based arguments before posting them to the discussion pages. The activity of defending edits in Session 6 (or, in the event there is no challenge to the contributions, declaring their value to Wikipedia) relies on students having developed skills for the composition outcomes listed earlier: possessing and employing rhetorical knowledge, critical thinking, and critical reading; utilizing open and collaborative composing practices; and possessing a knowledge of the accepted conventions for making meaning. By requiring students to reflect on their contributions and then defend their work with appeals to the improvement of the overall project, this session prepares them for professional audiences.

The last assignment stage, reflection, occurs in Sessions 7 and 8. Here students are asked to compose on their thoughts about the experience, and to channel those thoughts toward the course outcomes. The final reflection piece rests on the students' ability to assess the significance of their Wikipedia contributions not just in objective terms of how they might have improved the project, but also in terms of how the experience has changed them as writers. (If the student feels there has not been growth, the reflection piece can accommodate this stance as well.) Whether or not the student argues for development of their skills under the assignment—and most writers will point to a mixed record—Sessions 7 and 8 rest on the authenticity of the evidence cited. Practitioners of portfolio pedagogy will immediately recognize the reflection portion of this assignment and understand the comparison between a portfolio reflection piece (usually addressing the work of a semester) and the reflection piece of the Wikipedia assignment (addressing the more limited frame of one assignment). In either case, reflection is employed to solidify the development of writers by requiring them to highlight the changes in their practices and the significance of those changes.

While this assignment is not without its flaws, and is certainly not the only wiki writing assignment that could be envisioned to develop CBPP principles and composition outcomes, it is a good starting point. Within a reasonable amount of time, it will not only help your writers develop traditional composition skills, but it will do so in a CBPP format, which will encourage maximizing creativity and autonomy while best positioning the composition teacher as a coach. But while you now have an overview of the assignment, it is time to attend to the practical details of what you will face when you announce to your class, "We're writing in Wikipedia."

Diving In: Foregrounding Wikipedia as a Project Host Space

Start with the obvious: the first consideration to examine for this assignment is that the writing space is Wikipedia. But this reality is more complex than your students might first appreciate. For you, as a teacher, there will be some layers of preconceived notions to unravel to determine exactly what Wikipedia represents to your students. The same will be true for your students themselves.

As an in-class writing tool, Wikipedia can initially be contrasted with other collaborative electronic platforms; popular social networking sites such as MySpace and Facebook serve purposes different from Wikipedia's, and mentioning those other sites can serve as a way to start the conversation through discussion of what Wikipedia is not. The basic similarity between a social networking site and an open-access wiki is that student writing will appear in a much more open forum than most students are accustomed to using for the purposes of a composition class. Use of Wikipedia in the writing classroom means that you will be asking your students to write in a public space where anyone can revise or remove their text. There are fundamental differences in the technology between a wiki and a social networking site, but more important is the difference in mission: the most salient point of separation between Wikipedia and social networks is the fact that Wikipedia wants to fill the role of an encyclopedia, and unlike contributors to a social networking site, contributors to Wikipedia review submissions for accuracy and relevance to the core mission of the site. That review is famously problematic, to be sure, but it is also a more substantial readership for writing than your students might first suspect.

Thus, as anyone can and will review your students' writing to Wikipedia, you will need to prepare them for this fact. Students should enter the project knowing that they are writing for a real audience who writes back—and writes over text. Inform your writers early that your assessment of this assignment will not be based on how many of their contributions remain on Wikipedia over time. You are not asking students to compose a compare-contrast essay, place it on Wikipedia, and then wait to see if it is read or revised. Instead, you are asking them to generate writing that will fit Wikipedia's native format. Thus there is no need to camp out over their contributions and immediately attempt to revert changes other readers might make to a student "essay." Rather, your assessments will be based on measurements of the multiple acts professional writers regularly engage in: research, invention of their own text, review of their and others' work, editing others' work, individual contributions, collaborative contributions, negotiation of conflict for the greater good of the project, and meaningful reflection pieces about the entire experience.

While students need to be prepared for legitimate alteration of their submissions to Wikipedia, more troublesome, perhaps, is the fact that individuals outside your course might assail your writers in ways an instructor would never tolerate within the classroom. To be sure, most conduct between Wikipedia contributors is spirited and sometimes heated, but the aggregate tone is usually more or less professional. Vituperative assaults on a person run counter to the mission of the project and the most egregious examples are usually disciplined within Wikipedia. On the whole, these conflicts can be learning opportunities. The nature and number of problems your students will encounter when collaborating with their classmates and other writers on Wikipedia are an invaluable representation of the type of conflicts they will solve in the authentic writing environments beyond college. The opportunity to understand the project's goals, and to defend or judge contributions and edits based on those goals, provides college writers with challenges that not only prefigure their writing environment in the workplace, but also any environment where they will collaborate over electronic networks. Thus, you should prepare your writers for the fact that they will be writing in a public space—a new experience for many of them, perhaps, but given the pervasiveness of Facebook and MySpace, perhaps not.

Foregrounding Wikipedia for students is becoming increasingly difficult, since over the years most writers will have had substantial informal experience with this electronic source, now more than five years old. But like their experiences with word processors, your students' informal interactions may not have sustained a full understanding of the tool. Most likely their experiences with Wikipedia will have been through quick and informal Google searches, and perhaps via one of the top results listed by the Google algorithm. Thus, one place to continue your introduction will be to invite them to share their own initial experiences with Wikipedia: how did they first find it? How have they used it in the past?

Once you have opened the floor for a forum on the uses of Wikipedia, you will almost certainly receive anecdotes on Wikipedia controversies, both personal and public. Here are the most typical comments on a general discussion of Wikipedia, followed by responses grounded in pedagogical principles.

> *"My (teacher/parent/spiritual advisor) told me to never*
> *use Wikipedia, since anyone can write to it. And if*
> *anyone can write to it, it must be unreliable."*

You'd think so, wouldn't you? One of the best ways to address the credibility issue of Wikipedia is to present information available on four websites: *techcentralstation.com* (TCS), *Kuro5hin.org*, *nature.com*, and *Wikipedia.org* itself. The most famous case against Wikipedia is in Robert McHenry's article at TCS, "The Faith-Based Encyclopedia," which compares it to a public restroom in that one doesn't know who has used the facilities before (2004). Perhaps still more damning is the criticism of Larry Sanger, a co-founder of Wikipedia who left the project in part because of its insistence against what he terms "elitism." At *Kuro5hin.org*, Sanger makes the point that *"regardless* of whether Wikipedia *actually is* more or less reliable than the average encyclopedia, it is not *perceived* as adequately reliable by many librarians, teachers, and academics. The reason for this is not far to seek: those librarians etc. note that *anybody* can contribute and that there are no traditional review processes. You might hasten to reply that it does work nonetheless, and I would agree with you to a large extent, but your assurances will not put this concern to rest" (2004, emphases his).

You should counter McHenry and Sanger's viewpoints, however, with the thorough study of Wikipedia's accuracy conducted by the journal *Nature* using a blind-review system of experts. The study compared several Wikipedia articles to entries on the same topics in the online version of *Encyclopædia Britannica*, finding roughly three errors per *Britannica* article to every four errors in Wikipedia (Giles 2005). Thus, the online version of *Britannica* is more accurate, but not by much. It is also much smaller and much less able to revise itself.

Whether or not Wikipedia is as reliable as *Encyclopædia Britannica* online, and whether or not it has the perception problem Sanger notes, it is an electronic source that fills a need for many people. For the purposes of teaching composition, Wikipedia is an audience for your class's writing. Whether or not other Wikipedia contributors fail their audiences in their efforts to create a reliable encyclopedia, Wikipedia is an excellent platform for your students to begin to participate in collaborative writing for authentic purposes, since people across the world will access their contributions as soon as they are posted. Even as Wikipedia fails with some articles, it also presents persistent examples of success—as a final web source in this introduction to the assignment, you might present your class with Wikipedia's featured article of the day (on its "Main Page" at *en.wikipedia.org*).

Last, rather than rendering a final opinion on the worth of Wikipedia, consider keeping alive the debate over its value as a resource throughout the assignment. You will need to convince your students that there is enough credibility to the platform to employ it as a host for collaborative student writing—that's the threshold for your decision to use it in the composition classroom. But the threshold for its adoption and utilization as a resource for writers is a more intense issue. Encourage students to practice their critical thinking skills through developing their own positions about the platform and providing evidence for those opinions. As they become intimate users of Wikipedia, their opinions of its ultimate worth are sure to deepen.

*"My (teacher/parent/spiritual advisor) told me to never use
Wikipedia as a resource in a paper, since it is an encyclopedia."*

Teachers should feel lucky to receive this remark, since the appropriate use of Wikipedia as a resource in college writing is in fact clarified when authors ask themselves, "Would you use an encyclopedia for this reference in your paper?" Most assignments ask students to strive toward the roles of experts (albeit experts training) in their subject matter, and an encyclopedia—a first level of reference—betrays a lack of expertise when used in the place of sources accepted by that particular knowledge community.

This very issue was played out in the history department of Middlebury College in the winter of 2007. In reaction to students using Wikipedia as a source in history papers, professors in that department banned its use as a resource in academic writing. To the surprise of some, Jimmy Wales supported that stance: "I don't consider it as a negative thing at all. . . . Basically, they are recommending exactly what we suggested—students shouldn't be citing encyclopedias. I would hope they wouldn't be citing *Encyclopædia Britannica*, either" (Cohen 2007).

*"Why should we use Wikipedia in this class, if my
other teachers won't let me use it in their classes?"*

Here again it is helpful to keep in mind that there is a difference between the threshold of using Wikipedia for a collaborative writing project and of using it as a resource for a paper. When you address the two preceding questions, students should begin to understand that the utility and value of Wikipedia as a resource is itself an open question for the class, and indeed it is possible to entertain the question of the value of a source while composing for that source. Necessarily, then, students should know that they are invited to develop their own stances toward the resource. That alone should determine whether or not they use the source in other writing. It would be useful to ask students to comment on this topic at the beginning of the project as well as at its end. Similarly, asking them to ponder any changes in their stances on this issue would be fruitful for Stage 6, as would encouraging them to respond to this scenario: "Imagine that you use Wikipedia in a paper for a citation appropriate for an encyclopedia, but are challenged by a teacher for it. How would you respond?" Alternatively, students can address the same topic in answering, "Imagine that a teacher in another class encourages you to cite to Wikipedia instead of a print encyclopedia in your paper, but you disagree. How would you persuade your teacher?" By focusing on the difference between a collaborative platform and an authoritative source, students can both continue to develop as collaborative writers and exercise critical thinking skills.

"Don't people use Wikipedia to plagiarize papers?"

Though this might seem a rather bald question, it is not infrequently asked. Wikipedia's role as a lightning rod for issues of reliability and credibility in the electronic age are well-known by you and your students. Oftentimes less well-known is the fact that some of the multitudes of term paper mills online also utilize Wikipedia's texts, such as those summarizing commonly assigned literary works. Since Wikipedia's texts are not traditionally copyrighted, other sites pull from them wholesale, including *answers.com* and *reference.com*. Thus students may indeed know of writers who have plagiarized by stealing text directly from Wikipedia or by purchasing term papers that have done the same. But the error in logic here is the conflation of the crime and its tool. Just as we wouldn't blame a traditional encyclopedia for its unwitting role in acts of student plagiarism, so too should we refrain from maligning Wikipedia if a student chooses to use it for plagiarism, directly or otherwise.

"Don't people use Wikipedia to lie about themselves and others? If so, why would I want to get involved in that?"

In May 2005, a false biography of journalist John Seigenthaler Sr. was posted in Wikipedia. When Seigenthaler was notified of this biography, he contacted Jimmy Wales, Wikipedia's founder, asking that it be removed and that the contributor be named. Seigenthaler also wrote an opinion piece for *USA Today* about the experience (2005). Though the contributor of the false biography eventually stepped forward, Seigenthaler's false bio was prominently tracked in the media (see Wikipedia's "Seigenthaler Controversy" article). Since that time, biographies of popular, political, and/or controversial figures have been routinely used as vehicles for character assassination and résumé inflation. If students are aware of these incidents, consider that it might represent a healthy sign of their familiarity with current events. The answer here is that, while a largely public, online collaborative writing space can be hijacked for alternative purposes, the commons has policed these events in most instances, if belatedly. (In fact, the most creative response to date has come from a CalTech graduate student who created the Wikipedia Scanner to keep track of who is performing edits of selected articles [Borland 2007].)

> *"Since Wikipedia has so many problems with grammar, how will their contributors help me to improve my writing?"*

This belief comes directly from my 2005 class, and it is perhaps the most difficult to answer. Yes, it is certainly true that many Wikipedia contributors will possess a weaker command of language than your students. It is equally true that proofing work for errors—or, for that matter, any other editorial task—is not assigned to any specific person. It is also true that if another contributor gives your writer bad advice about his or her writing, there will be little you can do to address it if the student does not bring it to your attention.

The best answer for this concern lies in our understanding of constructive peer review practices in the composition classroom. The best advice for your writers is to approach their time collaborating on Wikipedia with persons outside the classroom as similar to peer review within the classroom, to the maximum extent feasible. Whenever a peer offers advice during peer review inside the classroom, the writer must ultimately decide if this knowledge is something he or she wants to adopt, and retains the ultimate responsibility for his or her own contributions. You might also point out to concerned students that the final product of the Wikipedia page in this assignment does not determine the entire grade of the project, and thus some of their fears—which might apply to a scenario of adopting erroneous advice for a repeated mistake in a term paper with no process component—simply do not apply to this collaborative assignment.

Many students will object to this model of learning, along the lines of the foundational/anti-foundational conflict so aptly explored by Kenneth Bruffee in his text *Collaborative Learning* (1999). Regardless of where students position themselves in those debates, writing teachers—whether working with wikis or not—always do themselves a favor when they recall that peer review is never intended for the sole benefit of the student writer. Peer review assists student reviewers as much as student authors, as it provides them all with the opportunity to see how fellow students struggle and succeed at the tasks they face themselves and contributes to a positive sense of peer pressure.

Instructors should keep in mind that they are in the process of introducing most students to a new concept—the use of the electronic network in the writing classroom. Traditionally, these networks have remained outside the scope of most students' academic lives. But there is one true marker for the moment when students have grasped and accepted the concept that Wikipedia will be used in their classroom. That moment comes when students ask how they will be graded.

Assessing the Wikipedia Writing Assignment

Once a teacher decides to create a new writing assignment, and is certain that it will support student learning outcomes, the first practical consideration should be: What portion of the final course grade will this assignment occupy? This decision involves determining the relative emphasis of the writing project. Wiki writing projects take a long time to develop: since the assignment is based upon collaboration, which involves greater intra-authorial communication, and since that communication will be a new classroom experience for many students (students will be used to collaboration on electronic platforms, but not necessarily with classmates for a graded product), the invention and revision phases of the project will require at least as much course calendar time as an individual writing project. If you are working on a 15–16 week semester model, and teach with a revision-based pedagogy, with four out-of-class essays, then a traditional essay probably requires three to four weeks of class time. A wiki-based writing experience will be no shorter than a sole-authored essay—our example assignment clocks in at just under 3 weeks, but in truth, if you include a peer day at the end of Session 7, your assignment will take up 3 full weeks. And that allows for absolutely no spare time. This does not mean that a wiki-based writing assignment will require 3–4 weeks, but only that you should make the wiki-based assignment roughly equivalent to the length of your current writing assignments.

There are two fundamental reasons for doing so: to give students enough time to develop the composition skills supported through the wiki assignment, and also to signal to students that this assignment is worth as much of their attention and focus as a traditional assignment. A wiki assignment with too little time will not allow students to evaluate potential topics, to learn how knowledge is made those communities, to evaluate what makes a worthy contribution to that community (both in terms of content and style), to develop expertise on the topic, or to share their revisions. Similarly, wiki writing projects are inherently process-based. As has been discussed elsewhere in this volume, wiki writing assignments blend the roles of writer and audience. In this assignment, the audience writes back. Therefore, students have to learn how to respond to their text being read and revised not only by themselves, but by motivated members of the wiki knowledge community. Thus, exploring and balancing these new roles will require at least as much time as sole-authorship essays, and likely more.

While establishing an adequate amount of time for the wiki assignment signals to students the importance of their work, there is no louder and more legible signal from teacher to student than the grade given for the work. Grades are the currency of the classroom. Thus, it is imperative for the success of the wiki assignment that you grant it the same amount of course credit in the final calculation that you would to a traditional assignment. If your essay assignments typically account for 10–20 percent of the final grade, so too should the wiki writing assignment. Many writing teachers apportion grades on a sliding scale, with the first essay of the course worth 10 percent of the final grade, the next essay of the same length worth 15 percent, followed by 20 percent, etc., so that students have the opportunity to adjust to the standards of the new course and new instructor; to receive assessment on an assignment; and to complete the create, revise, submit, and review cycle once through in order to make internal adjustments to the standards of the teacher as assessor. Since wiki assignments will most likely involve collaboration with class-mates, there is a compelling logic to placing them toward the end of the course so that students will be able to familiarize themselves with each other before working on a graded assignment together. Placing the wiki assignment toward the end of the course, however, might upset the linear progression of percentages mentioned above, unless the wiki assignment is given equal weight with the highest percentage assignment. Teachers who are experimenting with wiki writing assignments for the first time, however, will most likely want to keep the stakes toward the lower end of the scale since a new assignment always presents a teacher with a new risk-reward scenario, and until they gain experience with navigating its challenges, they will not want to "punish" students for their own poten-tial mistakes.

Once you have determined the appropriate weight for the assignment within your final grade calculation, you will want to determine how to assess the assignment itself, as shown in the rubric for our sample Assign-ment 4. There are some strategic points about this rubric that govern the assessment and therefore much of the assignment. These variables can be reset to fit any teaching philosophy, and an explanation of these choices will guide readers in the decision either to accept the rubric as it stands or revise it for their purposes. The first consideration of the rubric is that it does not directly assess the text contributed to Wikipedia. Instead, the assignment is more interested in the development and meta-cognition that leads to the invention, revision, and negotiation of the student con-tribution to Wikipedia. Session 5 requires students to present their edits, so the actual contributions are recorded within the classroom context, but in practice those contributions by themselves will make little sense without the context of critical thinking provided by the student writer. Teachers will also note that this rubric is split into two portions: an ana-lytic rubric for the writing portion of Sessions 2–6 and a staged rubric for the reflective essay of Sessions 7–8. Also key to the rubric is the fact that it weighs process and product equally. Sessions 2–6 are worth 50 points, and the final product of the reflective essay is also worth up to 50 points. Below is a look first at the operations of the process portion, and then the product.

Assessment of Assignment 4: Writing about Film in Public Spaces

Writing Stage Description	Points Awarded
Session 2: 10 points possible • Does the writer offer at least 250 words describing his or her initial understanding of Wikipedia? • Is thought given to the goals of Wikipedia and evidence offered of having conducted at least some cursory background reading on the site? • Does the writer describe his or her own opinion about approaching this assignment? • Is there reference to developing writing skills?	
Session 3: 10 points possible • Does the writer offer at least 250 words on the common rhetorical elements for 8 film pages? • Does the writer identify the elements required for an <u>adequate</u> film page in Wikipedia? • Does the writer explain what elements are required for a <u>better</u> film page in Wikipedia? • Did the writer consult the WikiProject page for films?	
Session 4: 10 points possible • In roughly 250 words or more, does the writer identify a plan for changes to a page using his or her description of the elements of a good film page from the last assignment (Session 2)? • Does the writer explain why those changes will both improve that Wikipedia page and further the development her own writing skills? • Does the writer reference both the five pillars of Wikipedia and our course outcomes?	
Session 5: 10 points possible • Does the writer include the actual edits made? • Does the writer format those changes according to subheading? • Does the writer include the four links to the page and talk page before and after changes?	

Session 6: 10 points possible

- Does the writer offer 250 words or more of reflection on his or her changes and their potential for improving Wikipedia?

Session 7 and 8, Reflective Essay Final: 50 points possible

Competent

If you meet **all** of the following standards, then your writing is at the competent level and will earn a score of 35–39:

- Essay identifies writing skills developed through the course and conveys an understanding of their significance
- Essay connects portions of Assignment 4 to writing skills, showing skill development (or lack of development) through the composing process of Assignment 4
- Essay integrates supporting text of the project page into the essay using appropriate MLA formatting
- Essay conveys an understanding of purpose for the wiki page as defined through its knowledge community and evaluates the writer's contribution on those terms

Skillful

If, in addition to the "competent" standards above, your writing meets **all** of the standards below, then your writing is at the skillful level and will earn a score of 40–44:

- Essay persuasively explains the writing skills developed through the course, provides examples, and conveys an understanding of their significance
- Essay persuasively displays development (or lack of development) of writing skills by synthesizing the various contributions to the wiki as well as the process documents of Sessions 2–6
- Essay coherently integrates supporting text from the wiki page into the essay using appropriate MLA formatting, evidencing a sense of professional standards and audience in both documents
- Essay conveys an understanding of purpose for the wiki page as defined through its knowledge community and evaluates the writer's contribution on those terms
- Essay displays an awareness of the epistemology of the wiki knowledge community and demonstrates successful contribution to that community, perhaps pointing to successful discussions on talk pages

Distinctive	
If you meet all of the "skillful" requirements above, and your writing stands out for **any** of the following reasons, then your writing is at the distinctive level and will earn a score of 45–50: • Writing reflects a sense of how knowledge is made and judged within the field • Writing participates in assessing worth of and/or defining its scope of project • Voice earns respect and exhibits trustworthiness for credible research • Contributions help advance page to acknowledgment within Wikipedia • Writer attends to issues that integrate other contributions • Community consensus on discussion pages acknowledges worth of writer's contributions • Writer shows extraordinary inventiveness and/or creativity in contributions	
Underdeveloped	
If your writing is lacking in **any** of the following ways, then your contributions are underdeveloped and will earn a score of 0–34: • Form of writing undercuts authority of writer and project • Essay identifies few outcomes, or conveys a failure to understand them • Contributions to wiki are erroneous, off-topic, or raise questions about credibility • Tone or quality of contributions to Wikipedia is inappropriate • Writer promotes conflict or exhibits less than professional behavior on discussion pages	
	Total (of 100):

The process portion of the rubric straightforwardly restates the writing prompts of Sessions 2–6. One weakness of this rubric is the fact that the process portion asks the instructor to assign a numeric value of one to ten without much guidance for the space in between the extremes. A typical analytic rubric would offer some way to differentiate points on the scale, but the rubric already includes a fairly granular focus in light of the fact that each row represents a stage of the complete writing assignment. In a sense, if the student has attempted the prompt, he or she is likely to score relatively well, since little distinction is offered between completing the task and failing to attempt it at all. However, when the analytic prompt is viewed with an eye toward the overall assignment, it still provides students and instructors with a clear understanding of the nature of the cognitive tasks, as well as the writing that will count as the evidence of that thinking. These first sessions are intended to support the Wikipedia contribution and produce the background thinking to assist the success of the actual contribution—they are scaffolding, in a sense. Thus, this portion of the rubric remains parallel to the session writing prompts, marking off a space where writers should interrogate their background assumptions and shape their texts for the needs of the project writers. As such, it invites open-ended thinking and largely equates success—at least at the process level—with the production of text.

The second portion of the rubric, for Sessions 7 and 8, examines the reflective essay as a product. Writers are asked to contemplate the worth of the entire assignment—orientation to Wikipedia, rhetorical analysis of Wikipedia pages, invention of text, posting of text, and negotiation of edits—within the frame of developing their writing skills. Those desired skills must originate from the course experience as a whole. Thus, success at this stage depends not only on having completed the Wikipedia contribution portion of the text, but the ability to integrate composition outcomes with the work completed within this unit. Not only will writers need to have identified these outcomes, but they will also need to have developed a feel for them if they are to recognize and evidence their application within their own work. Additionally, this portion of the rubric measures the ability of the writer to understand the knowledge-making conventions of the wiki and evaluate his or her own work within that framework. This portion of the rubric also measures the extent to which the writer's contributions are guided by an understanding of the purpose of the project.

This portion of the rubric is also a "staged" rubric—a combination between an analytic rubric and the holistic approach. The merits of the analytic rubric include its ability to spell out the specific criteria for success, but that very segmentation also precludes a focus on the overall effect of the text on the reader. Conversely, holistic rubrics privilege the overall focus but provide little in the way of specific feedback to guide writers during composition. The staged rubric attempts to combine the strengths of both approaches. It enumerates the specifics of the desirable writing it attempts to measure, but it places those details in hierarchical stages, thereby assigning a sense of their worth to the overall project. It states clearly the different qualities of thought, analysis, and reflection presented to the reader of the reflective essay, but it also differentiates several levels of success.

Why not evaluate the actual contributions to Wikipedia instead of the pre-writing material and the reflection? The first fact to complicate this more traditional assessment approach is the fact that on Wikipedia you cannot control your students' text. It might disappear. It might be amended by other writers, which would certainly complicate deciding how to assess a student's particular contributions. It is true that Wikipedia will list all the contributions of a particular login ID (under *en.wikipedia.org/wiki/Special:Contributions*), which is a great organizational help for a writing teacher, but in fact those lists are—for the purposes of a writing class—dependent on the surrounding text. Thus, to get a true sense of the value of the writer's submitted text, one would need to reconstruct a version of the page when the writer made his or her submission—not a task most writing teachers would readily embrace. Without the larger context of the Wikipedia page, there is no way to judge the worth of the contributions, and in fact there is little method for even reading the text. The writer's awareness about the significance of the Wikipedia contribution is the more valuable cognitive development; the reflection piece provides a space for that awareness to grow.

It is worth repeating that this is a sample assignment, and a sample assessment strategy. Each writing instructor will want to consider alterations to both the assignment and rubric to fit the particular pedagogical goals of his or her classroom. The key to making those types of changes lies in the connection to the outcomes of the course.

Connecting Wiki Writing to Composition Course Outcomes

How does a CBPP writing assignment support composition course outcomes? How would it help one to teach critical thinking, evaluation of sources, integration of sources, etc.? And how might a wiki writing assignment compare and contrast with more traditional writing assignments? Tables 2.1–2.4 are given in an effort to compare CBPP assignments like our sample Assignment 4 to traditional composition assignments as well as the Council of Writing Program Administrators' suggested outcomes for first-year composition. By situating the CBPP assignment next to these two paradigms, we can gain a better appreciation for what it will and will not accomplish.

Table 2.1 compares the approach of traditional assignments and CBPP assignments in their methods of achieving rhetorical knowledge outcomes. Developing a more meaningful and intimate understanding of the basic rhetorical motives—audience, message, and purpose—through writing is clearly a purpose of a composition course. Traditionally, we have asked students to compose thesis-driven essays in multiple modes for an imagined audience. In this format, instructors are asked not only to serve as the audience but also to craft the purpose of the writing assignment. Students do control the message somewhat, since they indeed will write it, but they must follow the often narrow parameters of the assignment. A typical example might be a compare-contrast essay where a student is asked to compare the development of melancholy in Edgar Allen Poe's "The Raven" and "Annabel Lee." The writer would offer a definition of "melancholy" and then contrast how each poem creates meaning for the reader by quoting the poems and arguing for a specific interpretation. In this instance, the audience is an imagined third party, but in truth that fiction is always much more alive in the teacher's mind than in the student's, since he or she wants to believe in the objective assessment of the student's writing. Whether or not the student believes in that fictional audience, he or she knows the instructor will assign the final grade to the project. And of course the assignment rather narrowly defines the writer's topic, or purpose and message.

By contrast, a CBPP assignment alters the fundamentals of audience, purpose, and message for the student writer. Following the principle of "laziness," the topic of the writing assignment is largely left open to the student. Rather than hitting upon evidence for a particular effect in instructor-selected poems, a student completing Assignment 4 has to decide which film to write about and what to say about that film, measuring his or her own interests, talents, and insights against the project's needs. This balance between personal motivation and professional need revitalizes the writer's sense of message and purpose, since the writer's decisions about what content to add to which project are influenced by the reactions of a real audience. Similarly, CBPP writing assignments fulfill the WPA outcome to "use conventions of format and structure appropriate to the rhetorical situation" by asking students to justify their texts to audiences according to the project's needs. Whenever a student contribution is challenged by a Wikipedia contributor, a need for a defense occurs, and students must call on their understanding of the rhetorical context of the overall project to defend their work. Tables 2.2, 2.3, and 2.4 extend the comparison of how CBPP assignments assist students in accomplishing differing sets of outcomes, including critical thinking, reading, and writing; processes; and knowledge of conventions.

Inter-wiki Writing and Intra-wiki Writing

The role of this chapter is to prepare its readers for creating and teaching wiki writing assignments, and while Assignment 4 has served as an instructive example, it does not define the fullest extent of wiki writing assignments. All too often, "wiki" is used as shorthand for "Wikipedia," glossing over key differences. In fact, Wikipedia is a particular type of wiki: largely open (with a modest registration, anyone can edit it), with the goals of an encyclopedia. It is a massive wiki—easily the largest— and well-established, but it is certainly not the only option for hosting the teaching of writing. There is a clear difference between wiki writing assignments that are limited to class participants and wiki writing assignments that capitalize on an existing wiki audience. Having examined the use of an external wiki—a wiki that is open to the public beyond the classroom—it will be profitable to contrast Wikipedia with some wiki

Table 2.1: Rhetorical knowledge comparison

WPA outcomes	Traditional assignments	CBPP assignments
Rhetorical knowledge • Focus on a purpose • Respond to the needs of different audiences • Respond appropriately to different kinds of rhetorical situations • Use conventions of format and structure appropriate to the rhetorical situation • Adopt appropriate voice, tone, and level of formality • Understand how genres shape reading and writing • Write in several genres	**Traditional FYC classrooms accomplish these goals by** • Asking students to write thesis-driven essays in multiple modes • Asking instructors to imagine, articulate, and respond to writing as if they were different audiences • Asking instructors to articulate and assess writing with appropriate voice, tone, and formality • Asking instructors to devise assignments in multiple genres • Creating peer-review groups	**CBPP-based FYC assignments accomplish these goals by** • Asking students to write in a CBPP format, such as a wiki • Asking students to write for different CBPP projects, with different audiences, purposes, and needs • Asking students in CBPP projects to justify their texts to audiences according to the project's needs • Research the CBPP project's format • Write for several CBPP communities

Table 2.2: Critical thinking, reading, and writing comparison

WPA outcomes	Traditional assignments	CBPP assignments
Critical thinking, reading, and writing	**Traditional FYC classrooms accomplish these goals by**	**CBPP-based FYC assignments accomplish these goals by**
• Use writing and reading for inquiry, learning, thinking, and communicating • Understand a writing assignment as a series of tasks, including finding, evaluating, analyzing, and synthesizing appropriate primary and secondary sources • Integrate their own ideas with those of others • Understand the relationships among language, knowledge, and power	• Assigning, discussing, and writing about meaningful readings • Integrating research training and opportunities • Practicing process writing, with stages built into writing assignments • Asking students to respond to others' ideas, either as researched or stated in class • Discussing relationships of knowledge, language and power	• Assigning, discussing, and writing about meaningful readings • Integrating research training and opportunities • Practicing process writing, with stages built into writing assignments • Asking students to respond to others' ideas, either as researched, stated in class, or stated to students in CBPP • Experiencing relationships of knowledge, language, and power editing text in CBPP

Table 2.3: Processes comparison

WPA outcomes	Traditional assignments	CBPP assignments
Processes	**Traditional FYC classrooms accomplish these goals by**	**CBPP-based FYC assignments accomplish these goals by**
• Be aware that it usually takes multiple drafts to create and complete a successful text • Develop flexible strategies for generating, revising, editing, and proof-reading • Understand writing as an open process that permits writers to use later invention and re-thinking to revise their work • Understand the collaborative and social aspects of writing processes • Learn to critique their own and others' works • Learn to balance the advantages of relying on others with the responsibility of doing their part • Use a variety of technologies to address a range of audiences	• Practicing process writing, with stages built into writing assignments • Employing limited collaboration in class, perhaps through peer review • Critiquing work of others through limited peer review • Discussing the need to rely on others, and perhaps performing that reliance in small groups with other students • Using a variety of technologies to address a range of audiences	• Practicing process writing, with stages built into writing assignments • Practice writing text in wiki "sandboxes" before committing it to CBPP • Experiencing collaborative writing in CBPP • Critiquing work of others, who respond to that critique, and then negotiate a solution to the critique • Relying on others by writing with others, and dividing tasks in CBPP • Using a variety of technologies to address a range of audiences

Table 2.4: Knowledge of conventions comparison

WPA outcomes	Traditional assignments	CBPP assignments
Knowledge of conventions • To build final results in stages • To review work-in-progress in collaborative peer groups for purposes other than editing • To save extensive editing for later parts of the writing process • To apply the technologies commonly used to research and communicate within their fields	**Traditional FYC classrooms accomplish these goals by** • Practicing process writing, with stages built into writing assignments • Reviewing work-in-progress in collaborative peer groups for purposes other than editing • Applying some technology	**CBPP-based FYC assignments accomplish these goals by** • Practicing process writing, with stages built into writing assignments • Reviewing work-in-progress in collaborative peer groups for purposes other than editing • Applying the technologies commonly used to research and communicate within their fields

platforms that could be limited to only class members, either explicitly or through lack of public awareness. This discussion is not intended to cover all available wikis, but rather to inform readers of a few basic options.

One such option is MediaWiki itself (*www.mediawiki.org*). Media-Wiki is the software platform that powers Wikipedia, and as an open-source platform, it is freely available to use. MediaWiki can be configured as an open wiki or it can be closed to only your class. Employing MediaWiki does require a server; currently server access can be had for as little as five dollars a month, and with programs such as Fantastico, installation and configuration of software packages has never been easier for the novice. While employing Mediawiki for a class project might seem like using a battleship where a dinghy would suffice, it is possible to leverage the robust capabilities of MediaWiki for a project that—though not the monolith that is Wikipedia—could outlive the class semester.

One such internal wiki was deployed in an advanced composition class taught by the author in Summer 2005. The "Letter from Birmingham Jail Project: Ethics, Rhetorics, and Southern Culture—Wired" attempted a more sustained rhetorical focus on a particular historical event. The wiki component was added primarily as a method for anchoring student research. Each student was asked to select a source or reference in King's famous letter, and then to create an encyclopedia article for that source, focusing on its rhetorical connection to the letter. MediaWiki was used to host this project, but while it was readable to the world, only students in the course were allowed to edit the pages.

Other wiki options that require hosting include TikiWiki (*tikiwiki. org*), which offers multiple functions beyond a wiki, and Drupal (*drupal. org*), a multipurpose blogging platform that provides a wiki module. There are many easier and simpler options, however, for instructors who want to use a wiki within the classroom but do not have the time, inclination, or resources to host a wiki site. Instructors should first explore whether the electronic platforms they currently employ already offer a wiki option. Pearson's MyCompLab and Bedford/St. Martin's Comp-Class are two leading electronic course management platforms that offer wiki functionality. Open-source course management platforms such as Moodle (*moodle.org*) and Sakai (*sakai.org*) also offer wikis. If those tools are not available, free wikis exist for anyone who can access a computer.

One of the most simple and reliable hosted wiki platforms has been PB-wiki (*www.pbwiki.com*), where teachers can create a wiki platform for one or many classes within minutes. Its motto, "It's as easy as making a peanut butter sandwich," holds true.

Putting Wiki Writing into Action:
The Composition Classroom and Beyond

In order to make the right wiki platform choice, instructors should have a good understanding of the broader dimensions of their particular wiki writing project. The following steps serve as a guide for designing a wiki writing assignment, and are appropriate for both composition classes and beyond.

- Decide what type of assignment this will be. Will it be limited to the students within a class (or several classes) on a limited-access wiki? Or will it be written for a public audience?
- Once the assignment is defined in terms of audience, then evaluate wiki platforms. If the assignment will be for an internal wiki, then consider wikis that may already exist on the electronic writing platforms you are using (e.g., WebCT, CompClass, MyCompLab). If those options are not available, consider wikis that provide hosting (e.g., PBwiki). If you are comfortable with installing and configuring a wiki—or are at least willing to learn—then consider wikis that you must host yourself (e.g., MediaWiki, Drupal).
- Consulting the outcomes for your class, write the assignment. Determine the specifics of the final writing product: will it consist of the actual wiki contributions, or will it be a reflective piece about the significance of those contributions? Then, working backwards from that final product, decide how many sessions you will give to the development of the final product. Consider sessions that will

    (1) introduce the concept of CBPP writing;
    (2) introduce the practices of writing on the particular wiki you have chosen;

(3) provide some time to survey the writing on the wiki, and to identify the values of that knowledge community;

(4) define the scope of the student's contributions to the wiki, and define the size of the collaborative groups;

(5) identify and define the elements of the best wiki pages;

(6) offer students a "safe" place to compose their contributions before submitting them, either in classroom drafts or in a wiki sandbox;

(7) submit student contributions to the wiki; and

(8) negotiate reader reactions and student revisions.

Each of these tasks need not correspond to a full class session. Depending on the emphasis you would like to offer, and your class length, you might combine several tasks in one day or break them across several classes.

- Once you have designed the appropriate sessions, you will need to design an assessment plan. Decide what should be low-stakes writing (e.g., process tasks that ask students to explore the wiki, record their impressions, make initial judgments, or draft contributions) and emphasize points for completion. Then decide what portion of the writing you want to emphasize as a finished product, and weight the assessment plan towards that product.

- Decide on the role of the wiki writing project in terms of the calculation of the overall grade. Which course outcomes does this assignment develop? When you consider what you want your students to know when they leave your course, ask yourself what role this assignment will play in developing that body of knowledge.

- Write the assignment. Provide a narrative introduction that you feel introduces the worth of the project and explains what it will do for the students in terms of developing their skills. Once you have taught such an assignment, ask the students for written permission to use their old assignments (with names removed) as examples, and include those examples in your current assignment (and if you are writing on a public wiki such as Wikipedia, refer to their old contributions on the site). Construct a calendar that provides development time for each of the tasks numbered above. Once you have fixed those sessions, construct a rubric with relative emphasis for each session.

- If you are writing for Wikipedia, register the assignment at its "School and university projects" page.

A CBPP writing assignment certainly presents some new challenges for writing teachers. As conceived here, such an assignment asks a teacher to surrender substantial control over student writing and the writing environment. But these changes in teaching practice bring with them substantial opportunities for student growth. Assignments that replace the teacher as surrogate audience with a genuine and engaged knowledge community demand not only a higher level of professional discourse from student writers but also a greater sense of purpose. The CBPP assignment envisioned in this chapter challenges writers to develop a greater sense of identity through a more meaningful connection with their writing as they have the opportunity to reflect on their own personal interests, talents, and desires before finding their entry point.

This assignment seeks to capitalize not only on the existing electronic networking infrastructure now commonly available in higher education but also on the social and cultural realities those networks bring with them, by applying the values of the composition classroom in the most useful environment. Writing for the *New York Times* about this very cultural shift, Alex Williams tracks the reality that the current generation of college students is less interested in traditionally prestigious careers—primarily in medicine and law—and the compromises to self-identity and exploration that typically come with them:

> "The older professions are great, they're wonderful," said Richard
> Florida, the author of *The Rise of the Creative Class . . . And How It's
> Transforming Work, Leisure, Community and Everyday Life* (Basic
> Books, 2003). "But they've lost their allure, their status. And it isn't
> about money." . . . It's not just because the professions have changed,
> but also because the standards of what makes a prestigious career
> have changed. This decline, Mr. Florida argued, is rooted in a broader
> shift in definitions of success, essentially, a realignment of the pillars.
> Especially among young people, professional status is now inextricably
> linked to ideas of flexibility and creativity, concepts alien to seemingly
> everyone but art students even a generation ago. (2008)

Bringing in CBPP writing is not an attempt to keep pace with job fads or to cater to some sort of whim. These trends in the job market reflect a more permanent underlying cultural shift occasioned by the predominance of electronic networks in our larger culture. CBPP writing assignments such as the one envisioned in this chapter attempt to capitalize on opportunities for supplying the composition classroom with authentic learning environments.

3

CBPP in the Composition Classroom: Case Studies

> I wrote a paragraph of text and there it was. . . . You write all these
> pages for college and no one ever sees it, and you write for Wikipedia
> and the whole world sees it, instantly.
> —Kathleen Walsh, Wikipedia contributor to
> "Contrabassoon" (Hafner 2006)

I taught two sections of first-year composition during the spring semester of 2005. In the fall I taught two more sections of first-year composition. All four courses incorporated wikis in the curriculum. In the Spring 2005 courses, I used a Wikipedia film page, "Memento," as the basis for the assignment discussed in Chapter 2. In the Fall 2005 courses, students revised film pages for Wikipedia as well as writing for World66, a travel wiki. The writing conducted in the spring of 2005 was not part of a formal experiment. What follows are the details of the Fall 2005 experiment.

My central question was whether or not CBPP can improve writing instruction. If it does, by what measures would we know it? I decided that I ought to at least attempt to measure fluency: how much students write for a CBPP assignment versus how much they write for a more traditional assignment. In the final analysis, the experiment yielded a lot of good information that will serve to guide readers who seek to attempt a CBPP assignment. But, though I learned a great deal from the experiment, from the outset the initial design was compromised.

Two primary methods of inquiry are available to researchers: quantitative and qualitative. Fortunately, they are no longer viewed as mutually exclusive in experimental design. This study collected both measurements, but the primary analysis is driven by qualitative data. There are several compelling reasons for this, but the primary and controlling factor was the limited sample set. This experiment involved only twenty-eight writers and almost no quantitative measurements from such a small sample set from which one can make reliable statistical inferences. To obtain a statistical significance against all composition sections at the university, this study would have had to look at more than one hundred writers to ensure that the quantitative measurements had not been affected by chance or unseen factors, and even a sample of that size would have been statistically vulnerable. Still, there is a need for quantitative measurement of CBPP claims. Thus, this chapter seeks to provide an overview of the writing produced by the students with limited quantitative measurements, and to employ qualitative measurements primarily through three extended case studies.

Experiment Overview

The course took place from August 19, 2005, through December 7, 2005. However, the experimental portion of this class was comprised of roughly ten days, from November 9, 2005, through November 19, 2005, during which student writers wrote entries on Wikipedia film pages. Composition occurred during class time as well as outside of class. I assigned daily short writing assignments that I read not only for indications of writing skill development, but also for any sign of abnormal fatigue or frustration. I also monitored student writing on the Wikipedia talk pages, where students defended their writing submissions.

Each section was comprised of fourteen students, an enviously low number from an instructor's standpoint necessitated by the small number of seats in the computer lab where the classes met. I introduced the experiment during class, followed by a question and answer session. I gave all students an outline for participation and extended to them the option of participating in the wiki writing component or completing a traditional writing assignment. Participation in the wiki experiment would not represent a substantial deviation in the amount of work required to complete the course as compared to non-experimental sections of the course. The course and experiment were structured so that students could meet all the standard outcomes of English 1101 whether or not they chose to participate in the experiment.

Initially, two CBPP sites were located for the experiment. Wikipedia, as a site modeled on the encyclopedia format, readily supports a corresponding traditional FYC essay grounded in composition pedagogy—the description. The second site selected for developing student CBPP writing was *www.World66.com*. World 66 is a wiki where travelers report their knowledge about localities and their experiences either as visitors or natives. Thus, it supported a corresponding traditional composition essay—description—but based specifically on a geographical place. Unfortunately for this experiment, World66's website software was not as sophisticated as MediaWiki, the underlying software of Wikipedia, and student entries were very difficult to trace. Once students posted work to World66, it became prohibitively difficult to track the contributions back to the individual. Due to the oversight of the researcher, these results were essentially lost to the experiment. In contrast, work submitted to Wikipedia is subsequently identifiable by contributor, through its robust combination of a contributions page (displaying contributions by individual) as well as a "track changes" feature (which allows the user to compare any two versions of a page). Therefore, only CBPP writing on the Wikipedia site produced easily accessed quantitative results.

The assignments for the experiment were designed as film essays. Essay 3 is a traditional essay: the student writer is asked to compose a sole-authored critical essay for readers who are already familiar with a film but have not yet solidified their evaluation of it. Essay 4, however, is similar to the Wikipedia film page project from Chapter 2: the work is collaborative and asks students to describe and document the work in an encyclopedic fashion.

Essay 3: Critical Film Essay

A film review is an article that is written for people who haven't seen a movie. It attempts to recommend whether or not they should see the film. Conversely, a theoretical essay assumes that its audience not only has seen the film at hand, but has also given it some thought. It assumes that the reader has a great deal of knowledge about specific films, movements in film, the careers of directors, etc. Your essay, the critical essay, is positioned somewhere between these two. For your essay you should assume that your audience is at least familiar with your film, but has not thought about it as extensively as you have. You might want to remind the reader about key themes or elements of the plot, but you do not need to dwell on repeating the film on paper.

What you do want to do is think about how the film works as a film. What is, in your mind, the most important aspect of the film? Once you have decided that (and that may take a while—several viewings), you need to pay attention to how the film accomplishes conveying that most important aspect to its viewer. For instance, if you decide that the most important aspect of the film *Dead Man Walking* is its ability to strike a balance between extreme positions in the capital punishment debate, then you might think about how the film does this: by presenting the foibles and mistakes of Sr. Mary Helen Prejean, by giving dialogue to both victims' families and the criminal's family, and by balancing the unsentimental dramatization of the state-sanctioned killing of a human being against reenactments of the crimes of the condemned. How does the film get its message across?

First, select the film you may want to write about. Choose a film as soon as possible from the list below that you can rent/access at the library for at least a week. Then, watch and digest the film.

Be prepared to watch this film several times, at least once before you begin writing in-class. THIS WILL TAKE A LOT OF YOUR TIME. (Sometimes students think writing about film is easier than writing about text, but you may be unpleasantly surprised if you don't budget your time wisely.) As you watch, keep notes. For the first viewing, note which elements of the film strike you as unfamiliar or perplexing. Note which elements are repeated to emphasize a point or a perception.

Calendar

Mon Oct 17

Discuss film elements, analysis of film. Select your film from list.

Wed Oct 19

Text dialogue on film due. Post in <emma> as Assignment 3, Stage 1.
Film screening session one.

Fri Oct 21

Film screening session two. Post text dialogue on first section of in-class film as Assignment 3, Stage 2.

Mon Oct 24

Post text dialogue on first section of in-class film as Assignment 3, Stage 3.

Wed Oct 26

TBA.

Mon Oct 31

Mid-process draft due. In-class peer response.

Wed Nov 2

Concluding revisions due.

List of Films

[Instructors should provide a list of films here. Since qualifications for including a film in the list are very subjective—such as whether the instructor has viewed it and considers it useful for teaching—no list has been attached.]

If you want to select a film not on this list, you must first check with me. It should be a film that I've seen and that I can imagine you writing a paper about.

Essay 4: Writing About Film in Public Spaces

For this last out of class project, we will write a film review for Wikipedia, the online encyclopedia.

1. The first aspect of the project will be to identify, review, and assess Wikipedia's goals and policies to determine how our information can best contribute to the goals of that project.
2. The second task will be to decide which film you will write about, and whether you will work as a group or on your own.
3. The third task will be to examine Wikipedia film pages to determine the rhetorical elements of the best pages. How would you determine the best pages? You can look at longer pages, most revised pages, most visited pages, etc., but it is best to survey pages which are well-developed, and identify common elements of style. Once you have a feel for what makes a good Wikipedia film page, you can then assess the film page of your choosing. You will need to describe what you think can and should be improved.
4. Make your changes to the page. Write out the changes in advance. Be sure to register with Wikipedia, and log in each time you access the site. Also, send me your login information. Before you save edits, make sure to use the preview function to read through the proposed changes, and explain your changes in the edit summary box.
5. Lastly, once you have begun making your contributions to the page, be sure to document on the discussion pages what you are changing and why you think it improves the page in terms of Wikipedia's own style. N.B. There is a high probability that what you write will be changed by another person on Wikipedia. Don't get upset.

Overall, your mission here is rather similar to our first essay, which sought to inform the reader about a topic. Since you are contributing to an encyclopedia project, you won't be contributing "original research." Rather, your mission is to attempt to summarize the state of knowledge on the given topic. You need not argue a thesis. Instead, you need to convey an ethos of expertise on the subject.

Dates

Wed 11/9/05

Project overview. Wikipedia orientation. Determine group or solo status.

Fri 11/11/05

250 words or more: Write out a description of your understanding of the Wikipedia project, its goals, its problems, and how you feel contributing to the project will or will not help your writing skills. Upload as Assignment 4, Stage 1.

Mon 11/14/05

250 words or more: Complete a rhetorical analysis of Wikipedia film pages. Examine at least 12 film pages. Read them, and identify their common rhetorical elements. What makes for a better film page in Wikipedia? Upload as Assignment 4, Stage 2.

Wed 11/16/05

250 words or more: Identify the film page you are working on. Using your description of the elements of a good film page from the last assignment, what changes do you think your film page needs? Upload as Assignment 4, Stage 3.

Fri 11/18/05

Make edits to your page, using the procedures described above. Upload a link to the page before and after you have made your changes. Assignment 4, Stage 4.

Mon 11/21/05

Wrap up.

As Table 3.1 shows, there were three options for structuring the experiment between the two courses, Option 1 is the traditional method of arranging control and experiment groupings. The benefit of this arrangement is that it "controls" for instructor bias; if the instructor's presentation unintentionally privileges either the control or experimental version of the assignment, then it will be less likely that those results will be duplicated for each group, and at least one set of results will not be tainted. If Essay 3 and 4 are on the same topic, then the drawback for Option 1 is the sequencing of the wiki versus the paper assignment. In Option 1, the 9:05 class is allowed to develop expertise in the topic in a traditional research paper and then apply it in the wiki; the 10:10 class must attempt to write for the audience in the wiki while simultaneously attempting to establish expertise on the topic. If, however, Essay 3 and Essay 4 are different topics, then it becomes more difficult to draw conclusions for each group's wiki writing experience, since the wiki audience participation might not be equivalent.

Option 2 presents essentially the same choice: if Essay 3 and Essay 4 are equivalent, then both groups must develop expertise on the topic and report their results to the wiki simultaneously. While this is certainly possible, it is more difficult than Option 3. If the Essay 3 and Essay 4 topics are dissimilar, then it will be difficult to compare the writing experiences regardless of where they occurred, since they will be dedicated to different topics.

If the topic for Essay 3 and Essay 4 remains the same, then Option 3 allows for all writers to develop expertise before writing on Wikipedia. It also allows direct comparison between the traditional writing experi-

Table 3.1: Experiment sequence options

	Option 1		Option 2		Option 3	
	Essay 3	Essay 4	Essay 3	Essay 4	Essay 3	Essay 4
9:05 class	Paper (control)	Wikipedia (experiment)	Wikipedia (experiment)	Paper (control)	Paper (control)	Wikipedia (experiment)
10:10 class	Wikipedia (experiment)	Paper (control)	Wikipedia (experiment)	Paper (control)	Paper (control)	Wikipedia (experiment)

ence and the CBPP environment. Therefore, Option 3 was chosen as the format for this experiment. Data collection was comprised of two phases: a questionnaire and a focus group. Questionnaires were completed by students on their own, while the focus group was conducted by another graduate instructor in the English department (Anita DeRouen) to encourage candid responses by students. All students' names have been withheld herein; instead, each student has been assigned a number.

Participation in the data-collection phases was strictly voluntary, and not every student participated in both phases. Each phase was worth 2.5 points of extra credit, to be added to the final average of the participant. No student could collect more than five points of extra credit. Students were offered alternative extra credit assignments if they did not wish to participate in the data collection. There was absolutely no penalty for not participating in the experiment. However, all twenty-eight students elected to participate and granted permission to republish their work and opinions.

The basic approach of the quantitative data was to measure how many words students wrote in Wikipedia, and then compare that to how much they wrote on a traditional assignment. However, as explained in detail below, it instead became necessary to measure the number of edits students made in the CBPP environment and compare those measurements to the traditional writing environment. In other words, students' edits to a Wikipedia film page were compared to their edits in a traditional essay on the same topic. In designing the measurements, both writing experiences needed to be for the same class credit and on the same topic. Thus, we asked one of the two classes to write an essay on a topic to develop FYC goals as a control group, and then asked the other class to write on the same topic as an experiment group.

The writing topics had be suitable both for a FYC classroom and Wikipedia. Typical "modes" approaches such as compare-contrast and thesis-based would not suffice since the resulting essays were unlikely to also serve as encyclopedia entriesSince much of what needs to be accomplished in terms of developing skills for FYC writers relies on assignments that develop argumentation skills, and there is not a valid CBPP environment for argumentation skills (in Wikipedia, argumentation would certainly violate the "neutral point of view" requirement), less than 50%

of the writing time was available for CBPP experimentation. If a FYC classroom schedules four essays (as I did for my classes), and one set of essays needs to serve as a control while the other serves as an experiment, there is not room for more than two CBPP writing experiments during the course.

The Quantitative Measure: Number of Edits

A central claim of Benkler's CBPP environment, as well as the concept of "laziness" as introduced, is that not reporting to either a manager or a market allows for greater productivity. Specifically, because workers are able to select what they will work on, and how much or how little they will produce, they both examine their own motivations and apply greater creativity to projects. In terms of the writing classroom, then, writing for this experiment was created in such a way as to best test those two claims. What is the quantitative evidence of writing with greater productivity? And what is the qualitative evidence of writing with greater creativity?

For the purposes of this project, there are two possible quantitative measures for greater writing productivity: number of words written and number of edits made. These measures alone are not necessarily the most apt in terms of composition measurement. Certainly, they could be expanded to give a greater context. Indeed, research conducted by Nancy Sommers and many others clearly articulates a consensus point of view that holistic revision practices are a better writing strategy than those that focus only upon specific edits (1982). But holistic revision is more difficult to establish quantitatively. In order to understand how a particular revision affects a text, it is necessary to collect qualitative information, especially about the writer's intentions. Thus, this study collects both quantitative information about student revision practices (hard numbers about the number of edits student writers made) and compares them with the qualitative information about revision as recorded in the case studies (including thoughts on what changes were made and what the students had hoped they would accomplish).

The writers in this experiment were asked to write an essay with a maximum number of words, and there was no method for changing this word limit without fundamentally altering the pedagogical structure of the course—doing so would have been to place the writers in a contest to write the most words. Therefore, there was not much use in comparing the number of words written in the traditional assignment (Essay 3) to the assignment in Wikipedia (Essay 4). Further, the writers in Wikipedia faced a very uneven landscape for their texts: some writers added text to very well-developed pages, and others created entirely new pages. Additionally, some writers faced environments where other contributors accepted their words without much question, while in other cases students saw their texts removed from Wikipedia almost as fast as they could add it.

Therefore, the quantitative measurement that could be measured for each individual writer was the number of edits made on the traditional paper assignment (Essay 3) compared to the number of edits made in Wikipedia (Essay 4). The results are shown in Table 3.2. Before consulting that table, the reader will need a note about the structure of the writing sequence for my class. Each essay project consisted of four stages: text dialogues, exploratory drafts, mid-process drafts, and concluding revisions (the final draft). Text dialogues are composed as short responses to readings, much along the lines of reading journals. There will be a text dialogue for each reading. At the conclusion of the readings, students freewrite a good amount of text without much restriction on form; these thoughts are collected in the exploratory draft. Students review the exploratory draft for valuable ideas that they then take forward into a more formal essay known as the mid-process draft. That draft is peer-reviewed, and from that peer review the author makes final changes and completes the concluding revisions, or final draft. A typical class will complete this cycle four times in a semester.

At the end of the semester, assessments are conducted through electronic portfolios (see Yancey and Weiser 1997). E-ports have the advantage of encouraging student reflection about the value of what they have learned in the class and how the course has impacted their development. This encourages quicker transference: students who leave a portfolio class are more aware of the skills they have acquired and are likely to use them sooner. E-ports give CBPP classes the added benefit of allowing students

Table 3.2: Number of edits

Student	Essay 3 MP	Essay 3 Final	Wikipedia
1	16	12	3
2	5	19	30
3	5	5	7
4	9	12	5
5	30	38	1
6	9	69	8
7	17	35	29
8	9	10	n/a
9	1	5	10
10	8	7	12
11	3	7	2
12	3	7	12
13	26	28	21
14	3	17	5
15	8	13	4
16	11	7	6
17	32	16	11
18	11	8	9
19	110	13	9
20	9	2	6
21	48	16	13
22	11	7	24
23	8	13	14
24	61	19	24
25	26	15	n/a
26	8	12	n/a
27	38	0	8
28	10	10	17

to process the impact of multiple, discrete, heterogeneous writing assignments and assess them in terms of the class's stated goals. Since the writing for wikis can generate multiple pieces of varying length, e-portfolios are an essential part of assessment in CBPP classes.

Thus, the column labeled "Essay 3 MP" represents the number of edits made by students on their mid-process drafts as compared to the preceding exploratory drafts. The column labeled "Final" indicates the number of edits made to the final drafts as compared to the mid-process drafts. The last column indicates the number of edits students made to Essay 4, their Wikipedia page. For the purposes of this study, an edit was defined as a single change to the text. Therefore, inserting a comma is an edit and is measured the same as inserting an entire paragraph. This is problematic for many reasons: Making a great number of edits to a text does not necessarily improve it. Yet, the measure of an edit remains one of the tools we can use to form a picture of the amount of attention students paid to each assignment.

Looking at the data tells us that there is little correlation between edit patterns in either environment. The greatest number of edits made to any document was 110, made by Student 19 to her mid-process draft of Essay 3. Yet in the next draft the writer made only thirteen edits, and in the Wikipedia environment that writer made nine. Some writers were heavy revisers in each environment (Students 7, 13, and 24). Some writers made substantially more revisions in Wikipedia compared to the paper environment (Students 2 and 9), while some revised more in the paper environment (Students 1, 5, and 19). In fact, in many cases, it is difficult to see any connection between revision patterns within the different stages of the traditional writing environment. For example, student 27 made 38 edits to his mid-process draft and none to the final draft. These data are, by almost any measure, inconclusive.

While comparing edits between traditional writing environments and the Wikipedia environment reveals little additional understanding, comparing edits made within Wikipedia is a different matter. Table 3.2 provides a good amount of evidence as to what makes a successful writing project within Wikipedia. By examining the number of edits each writer made, one is able to get a feel for how active they were within the Wikipedia project. More importantly, this table indicates not only how many words the writer (or collaborative writing team) was able to add, but also how many of those contributions remained one month later. These numbers indicate not only how active writers were within the Wikipedia environment, but also how that writing was received. Based on the numbers, we can take a closer look at three individual projects using a qualitative case study approach.

The Qualitative Measure: Three Case Studies

Case Study One: Student 13

In Fall 2005, at the age of eighteen, Student 13 enrolled in English 1101. In introducing herself to readers of her electronic portfolio, she portrayed herself as someone who had enjoyed a strong connection to dance and music throughout her life and who, above all, had always enjoyed texts: "I learned to read at an early age. When I was two years old, I loved to sit and look at books, memorizing them and looking at the pictures. By the time I was four, I could read well and was already writing short stories for fun. So I've always loved to read and write." Student 13 was also an avid *Star Wars* fan.

Student 13 was easily the quietest student in the class. When called upon, she was always able to participate, but her responses were so quiet as to be almost inaudible. This had the immediate effect of also quieting her classmates, who had to strain to hear her speak. Speaking then, as she was, into a silent void with absolutely no ambient chatter to offset her utterances, she invariably modulated her voice even further downwards. This created a cycle where the listeners strained themselves further still— sometimes physically leaning toward her—which lowered her voice even further. My polite requests to "speak up" were always ineffectual. In her portfolio biography, she wrote openly about this reluctance: "I have always been a bit shy and quiet. I'm the type of person who would rather spend time practicing dancing or reading a book, than go to a social event. And I've always hated getting up in front of a class to talk. I'm terrible at oral presentations. I always talk too fast and quietly and get really nervous." Student 13 was clearly someone who didn't like to speak aloud in public places.

But she had no such problem writing in them. As is often the case, muted responses in one venue seemed to lead to compensation in others. Student 13 wrote over twenty contributions and edits to the Wikipedia entry for *Star Wars Episode V: The Empire Strikes Back*, reflecting her expressed love for the films. Her wiki writing experience clearly reflects the "laziness" principle as applied in the writing classroom: when she was allowed to select the topic for writing, in the context of the project's needs, her passion for the topic became a driving factor and her creativity was engaged.

The assignment asked Student 13 to break down the tasks of establishing ethos, assessing project needs, and making textual contributions, and then justifying those contributions. Not only was Student 13 able to articulate what she believed made a good film page, but she also developed a rationale for why those elements needed to be present (or, in CBPP terms, she addressed their relevance and accuracy): "I think that the more developed and thorough a Wikipedia entry is, the better it is. I think there should be a brief summary for those who only want to know a little about the film, but the rest should be thorough and informative so that those who are fans of the movie will learn stuff too."

After reviewing twelve film pages, Student 13 narrowed down her choices to "Star Wars Episode V" or "The Aristocats." She was able to evaluate both pages and see that there were areas she could improve. She clearly had a preference for working with the *Star Wars* page, but she recognized that the knowledge community there was stormy and less than professional. In the pre-writing of Assignment 3, she wrote that, in the discussions she had read, "Some people were pretty hostile and used profane language when people made changes to their work. I want to do *The Empire Strikes Back* but I'm just not sure if it's a good idea or not." For the writing teacher, dilemmas such as Student 13's are desirable, as they reinforce the development of professional standards and discourse. I counseled her and her classmates to follow their interests, but also to hold communities to the standards of conduct at Wikipedia, where personal attacks are definitely not allowed.

As other students noted in the focus group, writing for a well-developed or hotly debated topic in Wikipedia can be challenging. The writer must assess the existing page and look for "an opening" wherein he or she can contribute. Even this task of assessment demands a threshold of topical expertise. Before the writer can even address the audience, he or she needs to have enough factual command of the topic to appreciate the strengths and weaknesses of the encyclopedia page both in terms of form and content. *Star Wars* pages were specifically cited in the focus group as an example of this. As one student observed, "Your writing, you get to be kind of like an expert about it, which is also nerve-wracking because you've got people who might dedicate their entire lives to this one movie. Like if you're writing about *Star Wars*, people could get really offended if you write something wrong about it."

Even a cursory glance at the *Star Wars* pages in Wikipedia reveals that the students' fears were well-grounded. Not only are the *Star Wars* pages well-developed, but the question of what should and should not be included in the entries is hotly debated. User comments are often emotional and tense, with more than enough vitriol to fill a political campaign. For example, within the discussion pages of "Star Wars Episode V," a user named "A Link to the Past" gives an idea of the tone of discourse to which Wikipedia can sink when he writes, "Adam, don't tell me I have no right to fix this article. I have MORE right, because my edits delete bad content." A combative tone is not in keeping with Wikipedia policy, as is widely acknowledged by Wikipedians; in fact, Wikipedia keeps track of some of the more ridiculous conflicts on a page entitled "Lamest Edit Wars."

Thus, for any student seeking to write for a reasonable audience, Wikipedia can present challenges in both locating a home for the content and then making it "stick." In fact, the fastidious and unbalanced perspective of some of its discourse participants creates a solid argument for Walter Ong's strategy of imagining a reasonable and literate audience (1975) over the immediate and infantile one that the electronic environment of transactional rhetoric sometimes provides. On the other hand, while many of the raging debates on a Wikipedia page might seem out-of-balance to the outside observer, or at least hopelessly nerdy, consider that as a knowledge community working under the operating conditions of transactional rhetoric, the narrowly-focused and technical debates within the Wikipedia knowledge community are often no different from debates within other professional communities. For instance, the debate on the "Star Wars Episode V" page that was nominated as a Lamest Edit War centered on the following question: should the page acknowledge an actor who was not credited in the original film version but later credited in the DVD release? For this group, the question was a threshold for defining relevancy—an issue clearly identified by CBPP theory. One camp argues that an original document is controlling; another argues that the updated version should be the authoritative guide. Strictly in terms of form, then, this debate is similar to arguments on whether Jewish, Christian, or Islamic texts are authoritative, or whether or not a constitution or its amendments are valid law. Only the perspective of the viewer can determine what constitutes a vital debate about a life-defining truth or an irrelevant debate between *Star Wars* nerds. For a first-year composition writer, this can be a very challenging writing environment indeed, and successfully navigating the dynamics of the CBPP community serves as an excellent preparation for more substantive debate after FYC. While the low transaction costs of Wikipedia make audience response a more material factor in the consciousness of all writers, not all of the voices are unreasonable.

With a choice of which community to engage and where she would be most productive, Student 13 eventually decided to tackle "Star Wars Episode V," even though its community was intimidating. After making her contributions to "Star Wars Episode V," she authored the following entry on its discussion page: "I contributed some things on this movie page. I did: 'awards and nominations' section; 'music' section; 'quotes' section; 'budget/box office info' section; added to the 'radio drama' section; 'theme' section; [and the] 'setting' section. I added these things to make the Wikipedia entry more complete and informative. I hope my contributions helped." Note that she couched her contributions in terms of the overall mission of the project in hopes of protecting her work from removal.

In response to Student 13's contributions and tacit hope of approval, one regular contributor indicated that her work would even influence the layout of other pages, answering directly her question of whether her contributions helped the project: "Yes! They certainly did. Now we can apply that to the other five *Star Wars* film articles. The only thing is, we removed redundant (setting) or POV sections (quotes, theme). Everything else is fine. This article was severely lacking in content, and your contributions helped quite a bit, from what I can see." The reference to "POV" (point of view) suggests that Student 13's sections on quotes and themes were removed because they violated Wikipedia policy, which states that "all Wikipedia articles must be written from a neutral point of view, representing views fairly and without bias."

How? Here is the theme statement that the Wikipedian removed: "The movie's overall theme is good versus evil. This theme is portrayed throughout the entire *Star Wars* saga. There are also many other smaller themes that play a role in the film including 'strength over fear,' 'peace over anger,' 'honor over hate' and selflessness over self-centeredness." This text could hardly be considered as conveying bias. Identifying themes in a creative work is, to a large degree, unavoidably subjective, and the student had included a "themes" section only after her research of several pages indicated that well-developed film pages included this type of information. Her deleted quotations were content taken directly from the film, with no commentary provided by the student. If content from the work in focus can itself be deemed too "subjective," what contributions cannot fall under violation of the NPOV policy?

At such points of bewilderment, however, it is worth considering that Wikipedia does function largely as it was intended to function. Studies such as the one conducted by *Nature* demonstrate that while Wikipedia is not quite as accurate as the electronic *Encyclopædia Britannica*, the difference in accuracy is not large enough to dismiss Wikipedia as unreliable (Giles 2005). Although Student 13 did not contact me with any concerns, I did remind the class that from time to time it was helpful just to look at the daily featured article on the main page of Wikipedia. Each day a new article is featured that highlights the best work of the process, indicating that by and large the key of CBPP, low-cost integration, is at work on Wikipedia. By and large, contributions to Wikipedia are successfully reviewed for accuracy and relevance. The constant parade of model articles on its homepage provides individual examples, and the *Nature* study provides evidence as to the accuracy across the breadth of Wikipedia's content.

Additionally, producing knowledge within an epistemic network necessarily involves convincing others to endorse your contributions. Thus, as a practical matter, students were reminded in the assignment "to document on the discussion pages what you are changing and why you think it improves the page in terms of Wikipedia's own style." In terms of Benkler's CBPP, Student 13 and the other contributors to the "Star Wars Episode V" page acted as co-contributors to a project that reviewed their modular and granular work for both relevance and accuracy. Student 13's experience also played out in terms of James Berlin's transactional rhetorics, as will be discussed more in Chapter 4. Berlin writes that "epistemic rhetoric posits a transaction that involves all elements of the rhetorical situation: interlocutor, audience, material reality, and language" (1987, 16). Thus, the collaboration can only make knowledge through dialogue:

each party has an equal right to edit text in Wikipedia, so the only way to make lasting contributions is to win the consent of other contributors by matching the relevance and accuracy of your content to the project's stated topic, which is itself open to editing.

Overall, Student 13's final thoughts about the experience revealed a balanced perspective. In composing her summative reaction to the assignment, Student 13 specifically cited the moment where her audience publicly praised her work and touted its usefulness. But the success of that moment was diminished somewhat by her feelings about the loss of traditional authorship and the lack of control over her text: "I don't like how all your work can get deleted so easily."

In spite of her reservations, Student 13 decided that writing for Wikipedia was a positive experience. Her summative comments were a committed endorsement of the idea of writing in a CBPP environment: "I enjoyed writing in Wikipedia. I'd never even heard of wikis before this class. Now I think I'm going to find them useful for both educational and entertainment purposes. I had a good experience with Wikipedia and am glad I was introduced to it."

How much of Student 13's positive reaction of the Wikipedia experience owes directly to the specific praise she received from Wikipedians? Further, how much of that praise is due to the low transaction costs, and how much was strictly chance? The class as a whole offered differing opinions about the experience of writing in Wikipedia. Many seemed to look with mild ambivalence at the experience as an experiment, both in the literal and metaphorical sense, summing up the experience with statements such as "I thought it was like challenging to try to find a way to integrate what you've already written . . . our movie paper was kind of like well-developed, and it was kind of hard to integrate what we wanted to put in. And then as soon as you would put it in, someone would change it." Others continued to reject the premise of Wikipedia entirely, citing many of the standard objections—no absolute control over text, too many demands in addressing a large public audience, or lack of factual integrity for a source which any one could edit. Of course, the class could not avoid seeing the entire experience through the lens of an experiment, since they had signed Institutional Review Board forms agreeing to participate in educational research. This was unavoidable. Therefore, there was an implicit understanding that even though these were graded assignments, the fact that they were conducted inside the confines of an experiment determined that this was a writing project in some way "off the beaten path."

Student 13's positive experience, when considered against some of the more critical comments of others in the focus group, indicates that the increased audience feedback in the transactional rhetoric environment is not merely desirable in terms of pedagogy, but perhaps essential. The acknowledgment from the knowledge community (that the student contribution was indeed helpful to the project) provided a new level of feedback that was both similar to and separate from peer response feedback. A student may well feel a sense of accomplishment after receiving praise from a classmate during a peer review, but positive feedback from a knowledge community on a CBPP contribution develops a sensibility within the writer of having produced work valuable to a larger community and immediately recognized as such, creating the desire for similar accomplishments within and beyond the education environment.

Case Study Two: Students 22 and 24

Students 22 and 24 worked collaboratively to create a Wikipedia page for the film *The Color Purple*. Neither student was initially aware that the other was interested in working on the project. Each student approached me about working on the page independently, and once I informed them that a classmate wanted to work on the same page, the pair willingly agreed to collaborate. The story of their collaboration gives the reader ample evidence of the fact that CBPP projects occasion student interactions that might not happen otherwise. While it is conceivable that these two students could have collaborated on a project based only on their proximity in the classroom, their interaction might not have occurred without a CBPP project. Neither of the two interacted much in class, and both came from social groups that, historically at least, have not always interacted well at the University of Georgia.

Student 22 was a young African-American man from the Bronx, and a recent transplant to Georgia. His demeanor in class was usually reserved; he was quite soft-spoken and did not usually initiate conversation. As his biography revealed, the central event in his life was the recent arrival of a younger brother. Relishing the role of big brother, Student 22 gave readers an idea of his values and perspective when he wrote, "Personally, I did not have any inspiration within my life—up until the birth of my now six-month-old brother, Christian, who means the world to me. . . . Ever since the day he was born, I made a promise to myself that I would become the epitome of an older-brother role model. I plan on passing down to him all the fundamentals of life, especially emphasizing the importance of a college education." Student 22 went on to explain that he hoped to work in a health profession, and that he had spent a great amount of time volunteering in that field. Not much about his biography indicated the type of writer he would become.

Student 24's biographical background was almost the opposite of Student 22's. A white female, she wrote about growing up in rural Georgia: "I am from Newnan, . . . a small, country town, [where] I was very involved in high school. I was a Varsity Cheerleader, Class Officer, and a member of many clubs and organizations." Yet the two students shared three similar characteristics: enthusiastic identification as University of Georgia students ("bulldawgs"), anxiety about writing for a professional audience, and the wish to pursue a career in medicine. Given these diverse geographical, racial, and gender characteristics, it is interesting to consider how a passion for *The Color Purple* would unite them. As a film about a female African-American character in rural Georgia, it offered something to appeal to the life story of each of these students. Both students independently selected *The Color Purple* only after reviewing twelve Wikipedia film pages and summarizing their form and content.

Both students expressed some apprehension at the outset of the project. Student 22 viewed Wikipedia with a willingness to participate, but also with some apprehension about the reliability of the open content model: "I feel that everyone who contributes to this website learns a little bit more than they already knew. Wikipedia appears to be unique because the articles posted in this site are edited by the general public, which means that the validity of its work needs to be checked." For this student, reacting to potential criticism seemed to be an important challenge, right alongside evaluating existing Wikipedia content to best determine where contributions might be most needed: "I feel that contributing to this project will help my writing skills because it will help me gain experience in accepting constructive criticisms and using them to my advantage. I think that this project will also help me in distinguishing important from non-important information within an article because it requires us to critically evaluate an article to see where best information could be used. I feel like this aspect of the project will especially help my writing skills."

Student 24 had a similar outlook on the assignment, but she was noticeably more anxious about her ability to contribute, and that anxiety came out clearly in her pre-writing reflection. She specifically feared the invention stage: "I will most likely read my film's page and not see anything I could add to it. It will take a lot of thought on what to add and what I can bring to this film's review. If I can find useful information to add, I do feel it will contribute to my writing skills. It will contribute to them because it will show me that I can think on other levels. It will help me realize that this type of information allows some thought and not something I can think of quickly. I feel this will be the most difficult assignment, thus far, for me. Hopefully I will be able to find something to add to my film's page. I am very nervous about beginning this assignment."

In the next stage of their assignment, both students began to review Wikipedia film pages to find out which pages were of interest to them. After reviewing several, Student 22 developed some definite opinions about what an audience of a Wikipedia film page needs: "What makes for a better film page? Well, I believe that a film page that contains the basic rhetorical elements such as plot/summary, external links, cast/actors, and awards are always well-rounded and thus, makes a better film page than those that do not contain this information. However, pages that are too long and boring are not favored by me at all. Each movie film page should have captivating photographs on their film pages so as to catch the immediate attention of its viewers." Thus, he came to the project with a preference for a succinct outline as well as some visual rhetoric. Student 24, however, praised depth in her review of Wikipedia film pages. Her preference for "depth" in content seems in keeping with her earlier fears about not being able to provide sufficient material: "A good film page on Wikipedia would go into depth on the themes and symbolisms found in a film. Possibly remind the viewer of something that they might have missed the first time they watched the film. Some of the pages I reviewed showed how the film related to pop culture. Another category I think would be interesting would be mentioning what the film has done for society. Or maybe even what influenced the film to be produced. Although Wikipedia gives the basic information of a film, I think the pages would be more interesting if they contained information that is not so obvious to the viewer."

The third and final stage of pre-writing asked the writers to make choices about which page they will edit and what they feel will be the major challenges for them. Both Student 22 and Student 24 felt strongly that *The Color Purple*—a major motion picture by Steven Spielberg that had been nominated for best picture in 1985—was certainly deserving of an entry. Given his preference for brevity, however, Student 22 envisioned that creating the structure for this page out of nothing would be a major challenge: "It is up to me to create a page that enables viewers to view the different aspects of the movie such as plot/summary, external links, awards, cast/actors, etc. Thus, this assignment will be especially difficult considering that I cannot make changes to my film's page on account of there not being one in the first place. I do feel like there is a lot to be said about this particular film and am astonished that no one online has created a film page for *The Color Purple*."

But it would not be entirely "up to him." Student 24 was at the same time reaching the conclusion that a page was needed for *The Color Purple*: "I have a lot of work to do on this film page. The film *The Color Purple* was a major picture film so I am surprised the page has not yet been produced. . . . I still need to do a lot of research about this film so I know in which direction my page is going to be geared towards." Both of these writers' statements indicated that the CBPP project had engaged them beyond the commitment of a traditional FYC writing assignment. They both expressed a sense of surprise that the page did not yet exist, as well as a sense of urgency about remedying that fact. They clearly understood that there was an audience for their work, and that the page would need to be both readable and reliable. There was no need for them to guess what their instructor wanted them to "write about," either, they themselves having researched the purpose of the Wikipedia project. Regardless of whether or not these students succeeded in developing a model Wikipedia page, they would be intensely connected to work that embodied all of the goals of the WPA Outcomes Statement for First-Year Composition: they would be developing a rhetorical knowledge of how to write to different audiences for different purposes, they would be synthesizing information from several sources and interpreting it for their audiences, they would be learning the conventions of a rhetorical community, and they would be engaging all of these tasks in an atmosphere of collaboration—one that dwarfed in scale the types of collaboration that had been previously possible inside the walls of a classroom.

The resulting Wikipedia page, "The Color Purple (film)" is, by almost any measure, a substantial contribution to the overall project. The two students' page, at the conclusion of the assignment, contained an introduction, a plot summary, a cast listing, a list of award nominations, and a section outlining the public reception of the film, as well as subheadings for "Themes," "Conflicts," and "External Links." These headings were developed by the two students after their own review of Wikipedia film pages, as well as after class discussion about similar reviews. Since the page was created by Student 24, there was no existing Wikipedia content to review before adding material. Both writers documented their entries on the discussion page, offering rationales for their contributions. Students 22 and 24 each made twenty-four edits to the page during the assignment period in November 2005, together contributing 801 words.

Only a few days after Students 22 and 24 created *The Color Purple* page, however, another user removed entire sections of their content—namely the "Conflicts," "Themes," and "Controversy and Public Reception" sections. Wikipedia etiquette asks that when users remove another's contributions, they attempt to discuss the matter on the talk pages. Good form also asks that users leave notes indicating the reason for their edits as they make them. The user who removed these sections, "SamuelWantman," was an experienced Wikipedia user, but he did not leave comments on the discussion page to expand upon his reasoning. He did indicate in his edit notes, however, that he was cleaning up the article and removing "POV."

Similar to Student 13, then, Students 22 and 24 faced challenges over the acceptance of their text by the network. Wikipedia defines NPOV in part by stating, "Debates are described, represented, and characterized, but not engaged in. Background is provided on who believes what and why, and which view is more popular. Detailed articles might also contain the mutual evaluations of each viewpoint, but studiously refrain from stating which is better. One can think of unbiased writing as the cold, fair, analytical description of all relevant sides of a debate." Each of the deleted sections had attempted to do just that—to summarize conflicts and state the positions held on each side. There had been portions of these passages that could have been read as judgments; for instance, in describing the controversy Spielberg faced over the possible inclusion of an explicitly lesbian love scene, our students had written, "The director, Steven Spielberg, had to be sure he portrayed the characters in the film in the same way one who had read the novel would picture them," a statement that would have needed some verification. But while some of the content in those sections might have infringed on either the NPOV or "No original research" policies, the section headings themselves had not. This one particular edit was overzealous if for no other reason than it removed three entire categories of information about the film, rather than the infringing statements themselves. This would not be significant if it were not a pattern: of the several writers who had substantial content removed from Wikipedia, most had sections removed in a similar manner.

More interesting, however, was the deletion of a quotes section. Student 24 added the quotes section to the page but Student 22 removed it. Within the entire class project, this was the only substantial example of a student from within the class removing the work of another student. Truly, it marks the fullest assimilation of a writer into the network: often, when student text had been removed from Wikipedia, students emotionally supported each other, often fostering an "us versus them" mentality from within the class. In this instance of intra-class editing, however, Student 22 followed the editing policy by at least offering the reasoning for his choice in the talk pages by writing, "I felt like the Quotes section that was on this page seemed to not serve much importance to the page overall, and as a result, I omitted it." Not much, if any, cross-talk occurred between Students 22 and 24 about these changes. The significance of the deletion of the film page's quotes section is that it marks a level of collaboration within the network that is often difficult to reach in the composition classroom itself: Traditional peer review, when conducted in a face-to-face environment, offers almost no incentive for students to risk offending others by deleting their text. The experience of these two writers authoring a collaborative document in a CBPP network offers evidence that perhaps removal of physical proximity, combined with a strong sense of purpose and audience demand in a CBPP network, allows writers to make more critical, challenging choices about shared text.

Student 22 indicated as much on his questionnaire. He wrote that "writing for Wikipedia actually encourages me to write because I find it to be extremely interesting for other people to edit my work. I like to look at the revisions and see where my writing lacked information or how I can better convey it." Thus, it should not come as a complete surprise that as a writer he found no problem breaking through the "politeness" barrier that hampers so many in-class peer-editing sessions and edited out Student 24's "quotes" section from "The Color Purple" page. Still, in spite of his positive contributions to Wikipedia and his successful editing experiences—or perhaps because of them—this student also did not seem to value Wikipedia as a resource. When asked if he would use the source in the future, Student 22 responded, "I would not necessarily say that Wikipedia is a valuable resource for me considering the very important detail that anyone can edit the information found on the site. If I were to use Wikipedia as a resource, I would first have to make sure that the information is correct. To me, it seems like a waste of time because I feel like I would be researching information that is thought to have been correct. I do not think that I would be likely to cite it in my research in the future."

This response is telling, since generally speaking, Student 22's writing experience on Wikipedia could be characterized as positive—he and Student 24 had created an article and contributed 801 words, and roughly one month later 87 percent of them (698 words) remained on the website, which would seem to indicate that their contributions were valued by the Wikipedia community. Perhaps some of this tendency to undervalue the experience lay in his perception of the difference between composing for Wikipedia and writing within a more traditional format. Student 22 has an interesting conception of the differences. In his characterization of the traditional classroom writing format, he added evidence concerning the difficulty of teaching students to envision and write for a professional audience, allowing the writing instructor to act as proxy. He stated the case more baldly when he wrote, "I feel that when writing in Wikipedia, you have to write for the general public. By doing so, you have to ensure that all your information is correct and unbiased. Most importantly, you have to be extremely careful not to include any information that would offend others. However, when writing a traditional academic paper, one may be reluctant to take these aspects into consideration because they are only writing for themselves and the professor. . . . I feel that there are a lot of guidelines to follow when writing in Wikipedia as opposed to writing a traditional academic paper, where the only guidelines the writer may be taking into consideration is those set forth by his/her professor."

Thus, referring to the traditional writing classroom, he specifically invokes as audience the writing instructor alone. In addition to giving no indication that the instructor reflects the values, needs, and demands of a professional audience, Student 22 not only declares that he writes only for the teacher, but in fact that doing so is less demanding than writing for a general public! Not only does Student 22 feel the pressure of ensuring that all of his "information is correct and unbiased" when writing for Wikipedia, but presumably he does not trust others to do the same. More commentary points out that perhaps Student 22, despite his success working in the Wikipedia environment, shares what Bruffee dubs the foundationalist approach.

Bruffee's *Collaborative Learning: Higher Education, Interdependence, and the Authority of Knowledge* is important for understanding CBPP in the composition classroom, and learning how to predict and defuse negative student reactions to an anti-foundationalist approach to learning. To characterize the foundationalist approach to learning, Bruffee tells the story of Zelda, a student in a class taught by David L. Rubin at the University of Virginia. Rubin organized the class into collaborative peer groups, which were responsible for reading and responding to each other's work. Zelda objected, at first on the grounds that her fellow students could not possibly have anything to tell her that Rubin could not teach her. Her question to Rubin—"Didn't [he] think it was a cop-out for a professor to make students to do all the work while not giving any right answers?" (15)—clearly sums up the foundationalist resistance to collaborative learning. Similarly, not only did Zelda think it was not feasible for her to read others' work, but she complained when others granted her that permission. But once Rubin convinced her she had been granted the right to read her peers' work, she "exceeded his requirements 'by a mile'" (17). Eventually, though Zelda learned to work under the collaborative system, she never embraced it. Even though she knew that she grew under the anti-foundationalist approach, which distributed to her and her peers the same responsibilities of the instructor in assessing their work, she would have preferred to live in a world where that authority was exercised by an instructor who knew something she did not and assumed a level of higher responsibility. Similarly, students in this study who resisted writing in the CBPP environment often cited a preference for clearly established lines of authority. For these students, knowledge was something to be handed down from acknowledged experts. The idea of millions of uncertified strangers collaboratively producing knowledge, they reasoned, was anything from specious to obscene. Thus, Student 22's approach was not as thoroughly foundationalist as that of other students. Bruffee's study on breaking up traditional learning approaches indicates just how difficult it can be for students to abandon their preconceived ideas about what a class should look like. Student acceptance of anti-foundationalist pedagogical practices—if not full, then at least provisional—remains a vital precondition to writing in a CBPP environment.

Case Study Three: Students 16, 19, 27, and 28

The largest collaboration in the Wikipedia project was a four-student collaboration on the page for *Good Will Hunting*. The group was comprised of Students 16, 19, 27, and 28, who made six, ten, nine, and seventeen edits respectively. As a group, they contributed approximately 2,632 words to the article, and a month after their contributions were made, 2623 (99 percent) of their text remained. Numerically, then, their contribution to Wikipedia would seem to have been very successful. In fact, of the entire project, they contributed the largest amount of words to Wikipedia that remained—another collaboration, for the page on *The Patriot*, offered more content to the database, but much of their text was poorly written and more than half of it was subsequently removed. While the *Good Will Hunting* collaboration did not elicit glowing reviews from other Wikipedia readers, Wikipedia did, by contrast, retain almost all of its contributions.

Within this *Good Will Hunting* group, Student 28 made the largest number of contributions and also posted the most feedback in her questionnaire. In many ways, her experience is consistent with the general tone of comments most students left on the questionnaire: they were open to the Wikipedia writing experience, they were dubious of its value as an in-depth resource, and they were not always sure exactly how writing in Wikipedia helped their development as writers, but they did feel that the experience was something all students should try. Student 28 elaborated on many of these issues and gave a more detailed rationale for her answers.

In the beginning of her work on the *Good Will Hunting* page, Student 28 admitted that she was hesitant about participating. Her main concern was integrating content on the page in a way that contributed to its overall value: "At first I was hesitant about how difficult it would be to know what to include on the wiki page I was working on, and what to leave out. However, after the first couple of days reading and practicing how to use the wiki, I found it to be just as easy as any other paper. . . . Even though I was discouraged to write when I saw how developed my wiki page was, it didn't take long to get a feel of what I could personally write about on the page." The data of this student's contributions bears out her intuition. She was able to make seventeen edits to the page, which is one edit shy of the total number of edits made by her three co-contributors. Additionally, contributions made by herself and her teammates were kept by Wikipedia—with only small alterations—for at least a month, whereas less successful contributions made by other classmates were often removed almost immediately. Thus, she was able to contribute more to Wikipedia and to find the writing experience more worthwhile, as she found the site to be a resource worth her time and energy.

Student 28 exhibited a nuanced appreciation for Wikipedia as a resource and project. Her co-contributors, who all made fewer edits to the project, by contrast did not feel that Wikipedia had much value beyond novelty. Students 16, 19, and 27 wrote that they were not likely to use Wikipedia in their research, nor would they object if an instructor were to forbid them from using the source in a paper. Student 27 noted that he "would not cite [Wikipedia] for his own research," and that being forbidden from using Wikipedia in a paper "would not be a big deal to me." Like Student 28, Student 19 expressed concerns about participating in the writing project. Her reservations with Wikipedia stemmed from a perceived lack of authority: "As a whole I thought writing on Wikipedia . . . did not really improve our writing any because we were not critiqued on it. Even if someone edited your passages, you still would not know if it was a middle-schooler surfing the Internet and changing it for fun, or whether it was someone who was skilled in the subject we were writing on." Even though the text was reviewed in class each day, this writer's response indicates that she requires a direct value judgment from an instructor on her text before she can see value in the exercise—a perspective very similar to Zelda's (Bruffee 14–19). Thus, given the fact that in this Wikipedia experiment the instructor would not award currency for her writing until the conclusion of the experiment—and even then that currency was to be doled out partially on the basis of how those "middle-schooler" Wikipedians responded to her text—it is safe to observe that she offers multiple reasons for withholding from full participation. It is also important to note that, like Student 27, Student 19's reservations extended beyond the procedure of the writing experience to Wikipedia itself. She recorded that she "would not cite [Wikipedia] as a source." Similarly, when asked about the difference between using a source on Galileo (UGA's online gateway to subscription databases) and Wikipedia, she responded that "there is definitely a difference. Galileo is not a freewriting database; you have to write factual information." Student 16 did not respond to the questionnaire.

Interestingly, Student 28, who contributed the most to the *Good Will Hunting* page, had found Wikipedia to be a valuable resource in the past. When asked if she found Wikipedia to be a valuable resource, she replied, "I think I would use wiki to get a general idea about a topic I was considering researching. . . . I am not so sure I would cite [Wikipedia] in a research paper, but I would use it for fundamental research." Her ability to locate the value of the source on a personal level correlated with her ability to contribute to the source for others. Student 28 realized that Wikipedia might not be as reliable as other electronic sources, yet that does not mean it is of no value; she had the ability to see the issue of textual authority in degrees rather than in absolutes. As for subscription sources such as Galileo, she wrote that Wikipedia "is easier to navigate. So many times with Galileo I have a hard time remembering where I found certain sources. With wiki, it is so much easier to just type in my subject and find what I am looking for. I also like how Wikipedia has pictures and constant criticism and updates. Galileo may lead you to dated information on your topic while wiki is virtually being changed nearly everyday."

Student 28 was one of the few writers to characterize the differences between Galileo and Wikipedia in terms beyond the sole measurement of credibility. Her argument that Wikipedia is constantly updated—much faster than traditionally peer-reviewed sources—is one that is often cited by Wikipedia's apologists, but she exhibits original thinking when she sees its benefits in presenting graphical information alongside textual, and, perhaps even more compellingly, the asset of accessibility. As Galileo acts as a gateway to a host of subscription databases for the University of Georgia community, by its very nature it remains a polyglot; librarians have dedicated a great deal of time and effort to navigating its heterogeneous landscape. Student 28 was unique in her ability to see that an asset of Wikipedia is the ability to conduct multiple searches on the same site.

While Wikipedia's policies and structures were definitely described and studied as a part of the experiment, I conducted the classes in such a way as to specifically avoid debate on the merits or problems with the site as a resource. This was to allow students to arrive at their own conclusions about the merits of the site. However, in reviewing the data of successful and unsuccessful experiences in participation, it is clear that there exists a strong correlation between the writers' perceived value of Wikipedia as a legitimate research tool and their ability to find contributing to it a worthwhile experience for writing development. Whether or not students had strong feelings of support for Wikipedia or held strict reservations about the project, their writing was assessed and graded just as their writing for a traditional essay would be assessed. Therefore, one might expect that students' appreciation for the project would be flat compared to traditional writing assignments, and that since they received a grade for the work completed, that even if they had strong opinions about Wikipedia in one manner or another, the fact that they were receiving credit roughly equal to an essay for their work would be the most important factor in predicting the success of their engagement. Instead, it appears that notions about the overall value of Wikipedia or online writing in general strongly affected their ability to participate. Indeed, those that had foundational knowledge issues with the project voiced the strongest reservations and were able to write the least.

Additionally, the three students who contributed the least to the *Good Will Hunting* page—Students 16, 19, and 27 combined made only five more edits than student 28—voiced distrust of collaborative assignments. Ironically, their work product embodied the very aspect of collaborative writing that they cited as problematic: "shirking." Shirking is the term for what occurs when rewards are tied to group results rather than individual performances; in such an environment, some actors will calculate the path of least resistance and collect rewards through group results that are higher than what their individual efforts merit. When asked if she thought assessment in group writing was fair if everyone who worked on the project received the same grade, Student 19 wrote, "No, because some people put in WAY MORE work and others only join the group to get out of the work." Student 19 made nine edits to the page, compared to Student 28's seventeen edits. Student 19's nine edits were comprised of five statements made on the discussion page and four contributions to the actual film page. Of those four contributions, one was a hyperlink, one deleted a paragraph, one was an edit of two paragraphs contributed by another person, and a fourth added a paragraph of content. Although Student 27 expressed no complaint with a shared grade for a topic, he too expressed a preference for traditional single-author work. He made fewer edits and contributions than all but Student 16, who made six edits.

Thus, the work of the group was spread unevenly—Student 28 clearly carried the majority of the obligations. How does she feel about group work? She too feared shirking: "I would rather write alone and not in a group for multiple reasons. One reason is social loafing, students' tendency to put less effort into an assignment when they share work with others." But perhaps more profoundly, she expresses a reservation against group work beyond shirking, one that cannot be easily mitigated—that the voice of the individual, capable of originality, can be squelched too easily by the chorus of the group effort. She continued, "Traditional projects encourage independent thought and conclusions, while writing in a group may make the majority exclude one person's individual ideas. Also, I think writing individually is more beneficial to the student because their work is evaluated on their performance, not a group's (which I feel can be vague)."

In addition to facing tensions over group assessment and parity, addressing the challenges of integrating contributions with existing material, and staring down their doubts about the validity of Wikipedia as a sound concept, many of the contributors positioned themselves in response to the pressures of writing for a large audience in a wiki. Unlike before, however, comfort with this issue was not always a reliable predictor of the student's ability to write successfully in Wikipedia. Student 27, who did not have a great number of edits in the *Good Will Hunting* project, had specifically noted that he preferred the idea of writing for a larger audience through a wiki. When asked if it would be more rewarding to write the same assignment in Wikipedia or a traditional paper format, he responded that he would prefer to write for Wikipedia because he "would like to be criticized by thousands of people who view my work."

Conclusion

The most important findings in this experiment come from the case studies. The main finding of this study is the correlation between students' "buy-in" to the fundamental concepts behind CBPP writing environments and their ability to write successfully within one. Students who most seriously questioned the ideas behind open, collaborative, online writing were less successful in contributing to it. Students who found value within the Wikipedia approach found greater success participating in it.

This study had been structured specifically to avoid these issues; within class, not much discussion was given to whether or not Wikipedia was successful or academically sound. Rather than prejudice students against their own participation by questioning Wikipedia or reinforcing the fact that it was part of an experiment (and therefore itself not a part of accepted, mainstream pedagogy), I instructed students only in the methods for participating within the platform rather than in the reasons why one should participate.

In hindsight, having had such a debate might have yielded better results for this experiment. It is not clear whether or not such a discussion would have led to greater participation. Instead, it is apparent that (1) the concept of Wikipedia remains quite controversial, and (2) student writers' attitudes toward that controversy materially affect their ability to participate within CBPP systems. Ultimately, CBPP needs to be justified to students as a legitimate part of the composition writing experience, and therefore as a method for learning writing skills. Successful acceptance of CBPP principles in the writing classroom requires an effective strategy for introducing, discussing, and debating the concepts of CBPP (cf. Chapter 2).

A second key finding from the case studies, as well as from a thorough review of the underlying student questionnaires, is that audience awareness figures prominently in the minds of students when they compose in CBPP. At some points, this awareness causes them to write more, and at other points it causes them to "clam up." But almost every writer who completed a questionnaire, in addition to a clear majority of the focus group, indicated that they felt pressure from having to write in such a public arena. This pressure created stress. Sometimes this topic came up in the classroom, but not nearly as much as it permeated their thoughts in their written reflections.

If students are given a chance to voice their concerns, then they might be better able to approach the experience of writing in the CBPP environment, having exorcised their fears and established a framework of at least cautious legitimation for CBPP as knowledge-producing systems; they will see their participation within such a system as valuable and worth their effort. Students tend to think that if we ask them to participate in a writing experiment, then we are asking them to gamble with their own currency—their grade for the class—while we sit on the sidelines of the experiment with nothing at stake. In fact, we know that the questions of textual instability that Wikipedia can draw to the fore of the FYC classroom were, in fact, thoroughly predicted by decades of postmodern language theory. Students—even those more likely than FYC students to be familiar with the pitfalls of assuming stability in language—want to assume that you are a language expert, that your reading of their text will make it "right," and that graduating from FYC will be an important step toward obtaining that social imprimatur of the college degree. And, to be fair, we often want to play the expert. But we know, in fact, that despite our gifts and talents for teaching writing skills, and despite the hard-fought skills that students genuinely acquire from our classes, access to the Internet grants students the potential for a larger stage. There is no doubt that if they can successfully navigate the large stage of a massive network, then they will be stronger writers for the experience.

As the reader is by now well aware, CBPP theory (as expressed by Benkler) specifically claims that the advantage of the CBPP work environment lies with the ability of the contributors to select what projects they will work on, and how much time and effort they will dedicate to the project. Thus, contributors in the CBPP network have "bought in" to the premise of their own work. This experiment was designed to replicate this key fact by allowing students to choose their own writing topics. It erred, however, in not allowing them to "buy in" similarly to the concept of Wikipedia itself. If students had been able to self-select their writing environment as well as their writing topics, then the same sort of enthusiasm and potential for creativity that drives Wikipedia and Linux might have been captured in this writing classroom. Writing for a CBPP environment represents a significant departure from what most students expect when they arrive in a FYC classroom. The strategy presented in Chapter 2 attempts to address the need for a transition from their expectations to the CBPP writing environment.

One final consideration should be derived from this study. It is worthwhile always to remember that CBPP represents a particular instance of a broader shift in communication that, as these chapters have shown, has the power to affect our students in many ways. This experiment—dedicated as it was to exploring the potential of CBPP in the FYC classroom—represented a change to two of the students' four writing assignments, but the results indicate that the best strategy for incorporating CBPP into a writing class is a gradual approach. Teachers should consider altering perhaps one assignment to include CBPP rather than two. If teachers are able to accommodate students' need for both a gradual immersion into CBPP assignments as well as an introduction to the CBPP network that honors their doubts and fears, future CBPP writing projects in the classroom will truly benefit from the case studies in this chapter.

4

Inserting CBPP into Composition and Rhetoric Theory

How does "laziness" work? In Chapter 1, much of the focus on the economics of CBPP rested upon transaction theory. Transaction theory plays a fundamental role in examining the economics of the market model of production, the firm model, and CBPP. In economic theory, transaction costs are the price any economic entity (individual, firm, or otherwise) incurs for getting a product to market. For Ronald Coase, lowered transaction costs were the key reason why firms existed: he demonstrated that firms would exist for as long as they were able to offer individuals transaction costs lower than when they worked on their own. But when individuals could sell their goods to market more cheaply, then they would do so directly, bypassing firms. Similarly, Benkler's insight is that under certain conditions (granular work, modular work, low costs of fixation, low costs of transmission, an environment of public information, and successful low-cost integration) CBPP offers lower transactional costs than either the market model or the firm model. Transaction costs for CBPP are lower than in the market model because, as in firm theory, the individual is not responsible for ensuring that the entire product reaches the marketplace—he or she can produce a smaller subset of the entire product. But the firm is inefficient in that it creates a middle layer between the productive individual and the market—management—that undertakes the responsibility of assessing each individual contributor's creative potential and matching it with the market's needs. Benkler's insight is that CBPP allows individuals to self-select projects to work on, and that this choice carries with it an increased efficiency in transaction costs, presuming that the individual is best suited to assess his or her own potential aptitude for successful contribution to a project. In other words, no one can know our creative preferences better than ourselves.

Here is where the discussion of "laziness" enters again: the computer network culture that spawned hacker culture enables individuals to work for motivations beyond traditional pay. Individuals are free to pursue their passions, in part because larger productions are broken into smaller components over the network and the scope of any one individual's contribution—from seconds of passing attention to years of dedicated research—are controlled by that individual. Thus, "laziness" serves as a masthead for the particular set of conditions where individuals are motivated to work by intrinsic desires rather than solely traditional motivations. To the extent that this condition is persistent in our students' lives, the field of composition must embrace it.

The common denominator in all three economic models—market, firm, or CBPP (which gives rise to "laziness")—is that participants choose the model based on the lowest transaction cost. In terms of writing instruction theory, transaction cost is a different but certainly related concept. Writers are interested in reaching an audience with their messages and experiencing as little impediment as possible. This is similar to the economic situation described earlier, which assumes that economic producers wish to reach the market with their product with the lowest possible transaction cost. Therefore, we might look at the transaction cost of rhetoric as the measure of the impediments placed in the way of an author attempting to reach an audience. Of course, the difference between economic and rhetorical transaction costs lies in the fact that most (but not all) economic models assume that the producer is manufacturing a material good, whereas the writer's job is to produce text—a entity that has a material component, certainly, but is substantially different enough to complicate the comparison.

In comparing writing models to economic models, I suggested in the introduction that we compare the market model to the professional writer and the firm model to the writing classroom. The market model is similar to the professional writer in that the writer engages the professional audience, or the market, successfully on his or her own, responding to the audience's signals in reaction to the text. The classroom model mimics the market model of teaching writing in that teachers of writing assume the role of firm manager based on their skills as professional writers, coaching writers on how best to reach their market, or audience. Comparing the classroom model of teaching writing to the firm model of economic production reveals two principal weaknesses in current composition theory.

The first structural limitation of the firm-as-classroom model is that the instructor must undertake the impossible task of responding to students' work as if he or she were the market, or professional audience, and provide a reaction as he or she imagines the audience would. As a pedagogical model, the firm-as-classroom is fraught with a number of faulty assumptions. It assumes that the audience would, in fact, read the students' work, presuming that the writer has sufficiently captured the reader's attention through any number of rhetorical measures. When the instructor plays audience, he or she mimics the manager in the firm model of economic production because both roles require an individual to interpret the signals of the market and then make decisions based upon that feedback. The manager, however, as compared to the writing instructor, has an infinitely simpler task, as he or she engages a real market that, should it choose to ignore the firm's product, delivers a clear signal to the firm in the form of lowered prices, indicating that the firm's output is not valued and that it needs to find alternative means to impact the market. While such news might be distressing to management, it is ultimately superior feedback to what the writing teacher can create, since the failure to purchase a product is more or less immediate, measurable, and authoritative. On the other hand, if the writing teacher misjudges the effectiveness of the student's potential to reach an audience, then the student carries inaccurate feedback about his or her writing practices on to the next level of education. In either case, focusing on this transactional element of both the economic model and the composition instruction model reveals the problem for the composition teacher of imagining and constructing audience reaction.

Comparing the writing teacher's job to the firm manager's job reveals a second limitation to the pedagogical assumptions of the writing classroom. Not only must the instructor create a hypothetical reaction representing all professional audience readers, but he or she must then interpret those imagined reactions in a pedagogical manner to assist the student's development as a writer. It is impossible to separate these two roles. The writing teacher is always "interpreting" his or her own reading, no matter how objective he or she wishes to be. These reactions take the form of assessment, and even if they are predicated on principles of good writing instruction that have been clearly stated in the classroom, instructor reactions are clearly limited and homogenous compared to the range of reactions a large audience might produce. The writing instructor is faced with not only the same problems of the firm manager but doubly so, since the instructor has the responsibility of both imagining and then interpreting the audience's signals. But the instructor must also formulate the writers' assignments, which are premised on judgments about what that imagined audience would desire to read. Likewise, the writing instructor often selects writing topics for students, rather than allowing them to self-select based on the assessment of their own skills and interest as well as a sense of what an audience would value. In this classroom model, students are limited by the instructor's imagination, not their own.

Applying the firm model to the classroom model suggests then that the writing instructor is caught in a double-bind of transactional inefficiency in situating himself or herself between writers and their audience: he or she cannot hope to supply the authentic voice of a diverse, varied, professional audience, just as he or she cannot examine a student writer's individual consciousness to determine which writing project would best suit his or her individual development. In terms of transaction theory, then, comparing the composition instructor to the firm manager reveals that we are raising transaction costs by asking the writing instructor to both gauge and select the most apt writing assignment for the student and then also to conjure the audience's reaction to that text. Given that access to a wide readership is available to student writers through the Internet, our current pedagogical model simply asks the writing teacher to do more than what is either necessary or possible. It is no longer necessary for the writing teacher to act as a proxy for a diverse professional audience, for one already exists if we are simply willing to harness the power of CBPP and accommodate networked writing projects in the writing classroom. In terms of transactional theory, both economic and rhetorical, we can now say that a focus on transaction costs for the writer reveals structural inefficiencies in the current classroom model that limit writers' connections with audience and writers' possibilities in terms of invention.

CBPP provides the synthesis for appending the market and firm models of writing. In the CBPP model, writers are trained to maximize their creativity and productivity in constructing responses to the varied demands the professional audience, as both delivered and received over a network. Similarly, the instructor is relieved of the necessity to assess students' interests and aptitudes for their topic selection, placing that job in the hands of those best situated to address it and thereby improving the writers' invention process. Instructors are freed to counsel students as they devise and publish writing projects, applying their knowledge of critical thinking skills to the demands of professional standards. It has long been recognized that grammar is taught most effectively and learned in the context of genuine writing applications; writers are much more interested in learning about the rules behind pronoun-antecedent agreement when a problem with that particular rule of standard English has hindered their communication with an audience (cf. Hartwell 1985 and O'Hare 1973). CBPP allows for the expansion of that composition truth outward from the real-world application of grammatical rules to the entire sweep of rhetorical concerns. CBPP supplies an audience-specific context for topic selection, content development, presentation, and reader response, improving the development of each by reducing the writers' transaction costs and, in effect, their proximity to an audience.

Situating CBPP Theory: Post-Process and Post-Electronic, but Epistemological

For some, using traditional rhetorical concerns such as "audience" to explain the impact of CBPP in the composition classroom will seem a bit odd. Contemporary theory in electronic rhetoric is most often associated with the fragmentary nature of postmodernism, or theories that generally undercut more traditional approaches in an attempt to rewrite the contemporary rhetorical framework. Works that have attempted to embrace postmodernity and evaluate its effect upon the electronic composition environment include Lester Faigley's *Fragments of Rationality* (1992) and Jay David Bolter's *Writing Space* (2001). While these works seek to break away from much of established rhetoric by introducing the new concerns of postmodernity, a brief consideration of their main concepts will show that even as they resist the frame of traditional rhetoric in describing the current postmodern writing reality, historically embedded concepts such as author, audience, and text are often unintentionally revalidated through the introduction of a new conceptual framework that, in turn, depends on an existing framework to establish itself through contrast. Further complicating matters is the recent emergence of post-process theory, a specific reaction to the process teaching paradigm that has dominated composition pedagogy for almost twenty years. Yet, as its very name implies, it too must also lean heavily on existing rhetorical principles to separate the "post" from "process." As this chapter will show, the most effective way to break away from the established rhetorical metaphors of understanding and find the most apt theoretical guide for CBPP in the composition classroom comes from James Berlin's epistemological approach composition theory, which views rhetorical theory not in terms of historical succession, but instead organizes approaches around their self-professed practices of knowledge creation. This does not mean that in order to properly evaluate and situate CBPP in the writing classroom, we will need to break away completely from any of these theoretical approaches; we will need existing theorizations of the writer's relationship with the audience from established composition writers such as Lisa Ede, Andrea Lunsford, and Peter Elbow to understand better the composing realities of working in a CBPP network. Instead, we can follow transaction economics naturally to transaction rhetoric: the epistemological reorganization of composition theory, suggested by the observed composition behaviors within the CBPP classroom, presents a compelling lens through which we can evaluate and re-integrate together established concepts such as audience, author, and text, rather than demanding a new world without them.

Faigley's work begins by grappling directly with postmodernism as a comprehensive phenomenon and then attempts to assess its import for composition studies. Faigley posits that the key generalization to take from the many postmodern currents in culture, art, philosophy, and theory is "that there is nothing outside contingent discourses to which a discourse of values can be grounded—no eternal truths, no universal human experience, no universal human rights, no overriding narrative of human progress" (1992, 8). Further, Faigley adds that "what a person does, thinks, says, and writes cannot be interpreted unambiguously because any human action does not rise out of a unified consciousness but rather from a momentary identity that is always multiple and in some respects incoherent. If consciousness is not present to one's own self, then it cannot be made transparent to another" (9). This last thought is particularly disconcerting for the compositionist: it might be possible to surrender to many of the cultural effects and literary suppositions of postmodernism that Faigley outlines, but when he draws postmodernism directly down onto the business of writing specifically, chaos threatens. Most of Faigley's emphasis in assessing the importance of postmodernism falls on the loss of the sense of self. Over and over again, his overview of the impact of postmodernism mentions the decomposition of the subject and loss of the coherent self.

Faigley also emphasizes the loss of a definable subject in explaining how postmodernism affects the teaching of writing. He writes that "where composition studies has proven least receptive to postmodern theory is in surrendering its belief in the writer as an autonomous self, even at a time when extensive group collaboration is practiced in many writing classrooms. Since the beginning of composition teaching in the late nineteenth century, college writing teachers have been heavily invested in the stability of the self and the attendant beliefs that writing can be a means of self-discovery and intellectual self-realization" (15). Thus, Faigley envisions current composition pedagogy as being at odds with postmodernism. The attendant loss of self should, it would seem, trigger an entirely new approach for the teaching of writing—one that reacts to the demands of "stitching together" a sense of self from a series of disconnected bits. Faigley implies that informed responses to the realities of teaching writing in the postmodern age are inconsistent with much of current teaching theory and practice, and he holds out expressivist practices as particularly vulnerable. How can we teach the traditional essay as a search for the fullest expression of one's inner voice if we fully accept that there is no longer any such thing as an autonomous subject to utter that voice?

In many ways, CBPP would then seem to represent the fullest, most troubling manifestation of Faigley's postmodern reality. In the CBPP environment, all readers are also authors. In many CBPP projects, contributors write collaboratively, and thus there is no discernable voice of the subject and no autonomous self. All of the utterances are clearly fixed in time, with the possibility that any and all utterances might disappear at any moment. But traditional composition practices—even those based in expressivism—are necessary to navigate effectively the postmodern composition spaces of CBPP. In order to write successfully in a wiki, students need the ability to pre-write in a traditional environment—to journal and gather ideas in a format where only the author, or perhaps the author and the writing teacher, are the only readers. This writing phase is usually followed by a contribution to the CBPP space, which is immediately followed by meta-discourse addressed to the audience about the merits of CBPP contribution. And, in order to draw the fullest value from the CBPP writing experience, it is optimal to ask student writers to reintegrate the "bits and pieces" they contributed to the CBPP environment into a narrative whole, complete with reflection about the instructional value of the CBPP experience (the basis for our model assignment in chapter two). This collection and reflection most often takes the form of the electronic portfolio. Thus, in practice, CBPP—a most postmodern and electronic space, where all of Faigley's characterizations of disconnected self and loss of rhetorical roles apply perhaps even more fully that he would have predicted in 1992—relies on a sandwich of "modernist" writing techniques to surround the postmodern CBPP experience and to deliver its fullest meaning. While Faigley's characterization of the challenges of teaching writing in the face of postmodern theory are beyond question, the it would be a mistake to assume that teaching in the networked environment assumes a reflexively postmodern approach. In contrast, successfully teaching writing in the CBPP environment links us even more strongly to the history of rhetoric and calls for an imaginative application of traditional rhetorical concepts in the classroom.

Bolter's work leads to similar conclusions, though his focus has followed a much more inductive approach. Unlike Faigley, who begins by looking at the comprehensive effect of postmodernism and then drawing specific inferences about composition theory, Bolter is most famous for his close reading of the experience of electronic reading, which draws upward to larger conclusions. As expressed in *Writing Space,* Bolter's main idea to track how the physical context for the presentation of text controls the text's possible interpretations. Print texts determine the organization of knowledge, while electronic texts allow or even compel the reader to construct meaning by making associative claims for the text. Bolter writes that "hypertext in all its electronic forms—the World Wide Web as well as the many stand alone systems—is the remediation of print. . . . Where printed genres are linear or hierarchical, hypertext is multiple and associative. Where a printed text is static, a hypertext responds to the reader's touch. The reader can move through a hypertext document in variety of reading orders. Whether multilinearity and interactivity really do render hypertext better than print is a cultural determination. The question becomes: better in what sense, for whose purposes, and, as various contemporary critics would immediately ask, for whose economic benefit?" (2001, 42). Bolter continues to position electronic text and print text as "rivals." Though Bolter's analysis is far too comprehensive and nuanced to sustain this implied binary, the act of contrasting the electronic writing environment to the print writing environment is continued here. Such a stance, like Faigley's postmodern crisis, implies that teachers of writing who employ an electronic writing environment such as CBPP are forced to choose an attendant electronic rhetoric. Again, such a choice is a false. There is no reason why working in electronic environments should require writing teachers to reject or minimize familiar and established rhetorical concepts. As the experience of CBPP demonstrates, CBPP links us strongly to the history of rhetoric and composition and makes it possible to work with those ideas in a new medium and classroom situation.

Both Faigley's postmodern analysis and Bolter's new media approach would seem to force teachers of CBPP to choose between an older, established rhetoric of familiar authors, texts, and audiences, and a newer electronic rhetoric where these concepts are, if not abandoned, at least outdated. This study will do nothing to refute the idea that CBPP, as a new electronic phenomenon, will demand flexibility and novel adaptations in order to employ it effectively in the composition classroom. Yet the fundamental truths of written communication do not change because the communication environment has changed.

Berlin's Epistemological Classification of Rhetoric

There are several underlying assumptions in my proposed model of the CBPP classroom. The primary belief is that the role of the writing teacher is to prepare the student writer to interact with a diverse, public, and professional audience who shares knowledge and expertise about a given topic. The highest form of that interaction would be student writing that demonstrates critical thinking, subject knowledge, professional ethos, context-appropriate appeals, and a fluency of form and convention. By removing the writing teacher from the role of conjuring and interpreting the reaction of that professional audience, the CBPP classroom represents not only a shift away from current pedagogical norms but also an implicit move further away from objective and subjective rhetorical theories toward transactional theory as classified by James Berlin and described in this section.

CBPP exists because it improves upon the efficiency of transaction costs of both the market model and the firm model of economics; this truth also supports the use of transactional rhetorical theory in the writing classroom. As we have seen, the economic definition of transaction theory is dedicated to reducing the costs encountered by the seller to reach a buyer. Rhetorical transaction theory has a different but related meaning. Writer James A. Berlin identifies this connection when he offers a taxonomy of composition theory in his work *Rhetoric and Reality: Writing Instruction in American Colleges, 1900–1985* (1987). Berlin's approach is philosophical, or, more accurately, epistemological. He groups composition theories around the broad concept of truth—how each approach assumes truth is positioned, and how writers reveal it. Thus he offers three clearly defined categories for the various approaches to teaching writing, which span the entire sweep of composition history, and regroups writers according to their approaches rather than their historical period. Berlin writes, "I have . . . three epistemological categories: the objective, the subjective, and the transactional. Objective theories locate reality in the external world, in the material objects of experience. Subjective theories place truth within the subject, to be discovered through an act of internal apprehension. And transactional theories locate reality at the point of interaction of subject and object, with audience and language as mediating agencies" (6).

Both objective and subjective theories support the role of the writing teacher as the sole interpreter of the audience: subjective theories implicitly support it because they assume that truth lies within interpretation, and as such there is no improving upon positioning the most experienced writer in the classroom—the writing instructor—as the sole interpreter of the value of student writing and the sole conjurer of audience response. Objective theories also privilege the position of writing teacher as proxy for the audience since they assume that truth is to be verified through the exercise of writing that can be demonstrated to be "good" according to the application of a particular set of writing practices. No one in the objectively theorized writing classroom—not even the audience for whom the writing is intended (unless the teacher and the intended audience are one in the same)—can equal the authority of the writing teacher in his or her judgment of good writing. Therefore, both objective and subjective theories of composition seek connection with a genuine audience beyond the instructor with no particular urgency. Conversely, transactional theory is a writing approach that is vested in audience connection as a composition strategy.

Embracing CBPP does not mean, however, that we need to abandon all the aspects of composition theory that would fall under either the objective or subjective theory umbrellas. In fact, as we will see later in this chapter, the classroom pedagogy adopted by this study for employing CBPP borrows heavily from subjective, expressivist theorists Peter Elbow and Donald Murray, both to theorize how the arrival of CBPP reformulates the concept of audience for writers and to develop practical writing strategies for assimilating the writers' internal truths as expressed through their texts into the CBPP environment. Similarly, this same pedagogy contains aspects of objective, current-traditional rhetoric when it asks student writers to evaluate writing within in the CBPP and assess the needs of that writing by measuring how it does or does not live up to a singular notion of truth. When writers are asked to read multiple Wikipedia film pages, establish the criteria for "best" film page, and then measure those pages according to this yardstick, they are fulfilling the design of objective theorists by practicing a positivistic approach that locates reality in the material world—i.e., there is an ideal film page, we can articulate the ideal film page, we can measure the existing film page against the ideal, and we can make changes to the existing page to move it closer to the ideal.

Thus, while the importation of CBPP into the writing classroom revitalizes transactional rhetoric, it does not render all teaching approaches based on subjective and objective theories valueless. Importing CBPP into the writing classroom instead reveals the extent to which subjective and objective theories have thus far been privileged as dominant teaching paradigms, overinvesting the role and function of the students' audience in the writing teacher. As CBPP economic theory makes clear, we no longer need to rely on either a solitary connection or a firm-based connection to the marketplace to be productive. In the classroom, however, there had never been a viable market model of composition; instead, the firm model of teaching has been the only practical model. Now that CBPP clearly identifies that student writers have alternative paths to an audience and that the teacher need not attempt to always approximate a professional audience, it is possible to see other routes to an authentic audience that simply were not possible in the past. These new, networked approaches clearly favor transactional rhetoric.

In economic terms, transaction theory functions because it always focuses on the connection between buyer and seller rather than on either party directly. Similarly, rhetorical transaction theory locates its focus between speaker and audience instead of with either party. A rhetorical theory based on a strict interpretation of the economic transaction costs would focus upon reducing the distance, or costs, between writer and audience. As Berlin makes clear, transactional theories of rhetoric imply an awareness of multiple parties at all times as it locates truth between those parties rather than with any particular party. This perspective offers an apt fit for CBPP because its underlying structural network assumptions mimic the same structural assumptions of transactional rhetorical theories: CBPP is direct result of network structure, and transactional rhetoric assumes a communication network. By situating truth between communicating parties, transactional rhetorical theory assumes the equal importance of each communicator. Similarly, CBPP assumes a network structure, with communication between equal nodes creating content through the act of transmission.

Transactional Rhetoric, Linux, and Topic
in the Composition Classroom

The transaction cost theory of economics is dedicated to reducing the cost, or access, of the individual to the marketplace. Similarly, the application of CBPP in the writing classroom reduces the cost of accessing an audience for student writers, or, in more practical terms, thrusts them into the sphere of electronic public discourse. It is possible to develop a composition approach that both anticipates the needs of student writers in the CBPP arena and furthers that discourse to the greater benefit of all CBPP participants, not just students. This practical approach, however, must be rooted in a thorough understanding of the fundamental rhetorical principles at work within CBPP. To that end, Berlin's supra-classification of rhetorical theory known as transactional rhetoric has been considered. The concept of transactional rhetoric fits CBPP well because of the fundamental assumption of discourse between multiple parties seeking truth is similar to the equal-node structure of a CBPP network.

Consider more closely the three categories of transactional rhetoric for even more accurate support of teaching writing with CBPP. Berlin's three categories for transactional rhetoric are classical, cognitive, and epistemic. These three transactional rhetorics are united epistemologically around the idea that truth is located neither within ourselves (as held by subjective rhetoric) nor within external objects (as held by objective rhetoric), but rather through transactions between the subject and object. But each of the three transactional theories offers a variant on this common approach. In describing the contemporary application of classical rhetoric, Berlin notes that "the distinguishing feature of the version of classical rhetoric that appeared during the sixties and seventies was its commitment to rationality" (1987, 155). Berlin also notes that the main appeal of classical rhetoric (as applied through works such as Edward P. J. Corbett and Robert J. Connors's *Classical Rhetoric for the Modern Student* [1999]), is its coherent and comprehensive approach to each stage of the writing process, as well as its ability to emphasize emotional, ethical, and logical appeals (157). Thus, while classical rhetoric provides structural terms—such as author, text, and audience—for analyzing CBPP in the composition classroom, its classical framework does not go beyond providing the basic tool set for analyzing the impact of writing for a massive electronic network. In essence, classical rhetoric gives us the concepts for understanding what transpires on the network when it does not envision the network itself.

Alternatively, Berlin characterizes cognitive rhetoric as "distinguished by its assertion that the mind is composed of a set of structures that develop in a chronological sequence. . . . In attempting to understand the nature of writing, it is necessary to know the nature of these structures, how they unfold in time, and how they are involved in the composing process" (159). But this focus on the interior cognitive functions of the individual can lead one to assume that cognitive rhetoric is more like subjective rhetoric, rather than a true transactional theory. Berlin, however, anticipates this objection and offers the clarification that, "although the rhetoric of cognitive psychology focuses on the psychology of the individual, it is indeed a transactional approach. . . . Writing also involves a transaction among the elements of the rhetorical context. The structures of the mind are such that they correspond to the structures of reality, the structures of the minds of the audience, and the structures of language. Learning to write requires the cultivation of the appropriate cognitive structures so that the structures of reality, the audience, and the language can be understood" (159).

Thus, before one can usefully employ cognitive rhetoric to understand CBPP in the writing classroom, more research will need to be conducted to understand more fully how networked writing affects the cognitive interplay between the structures of the authors' minds, the structures of the audiences' minds, and the structures of the networks. Cognitive rhetoric is most famously associated with the experiments conducted by Linda S. Flower and John R. Hayes in "A Cognitive Process Theory of Writing" (1981). In these experiments, Flower and Hayes asked writers to think out loud as they engaged in different writing tasks, including pre-writing and composing. While this one set of experiments in no way defines the entire field of cognitive rhetoric, it does reveal the key fact that in order to draw inferences about the structure of authors' minds, the structure of language, and the structure of audiences' minds, it is essential to design an experiment with representative protocol in place. Thus, for cognitive rhetoric to contribute to our understanding of how to teach writing with

CBPP, theorists will need to experiment with CBPP networks explicitly. It is encouraging that some of this type of exciting research is currently underway in the newly emerging interdisciplinary field of "distributed cognition" (Paré 2000), but at the moment, there is very little research in the field of cognitive rhetoric that advises how to teach writing using a CBPP network.

Epistemic rhetoric, however, is readily adapted to inform teaching writing with a CBPP system. In defining epistemic rhetoric, Berlin writes: "Rhetoric exists not merely so that truth may be communicated: rhetoric exists so that truth may be discovered. The epistemic position implies that knowledge is not discovered by reason alone, that cognitive and affective processes are not separate, that intersubjectivity is the condition of all knowledge, and that the contact of minds affects knowledge" (1987, 165). The importance of this position in understanding CBPP cannot be underestimated. If the discovery of knowledge is affected by the number of minds that come into contact with it, then there first must be multiple minds to contribute to the conversation. Knowledge is thus a product of a conversation between parties, and the more parties in that conversation, the greater the potential. Therefore the fundamental premise of epistemic rhetoric is that an effective knowledge-making strategy needs multiple participants. Composition pedagogy that is structurally designed to maximize multiple conversations among multiple participants offers the surest approach for writers to discover and contribute to new knowledge. Wikis such as Wikipedia, which present knowledge collaboratively, offer the most obvious example of an epistemic network.

However, the most accomplished example of an epistemic network is the Linux project, which began when an individual, Linus Torvalds, took a computer coding project that he had been developing on his own in MINIX and solicited help from other people. He did this by starting a public conversation in an electronic arena: specifically, he posted a message on a MINIX discussion group (Torvalds 1991). Other participants in the group had self-identified as being interested in the MINIX topic, and thus he had a ready discourse community. The project that Torvalds and others would "fork" into Linux qualifies as CBPP since it met all of Benkler's criteria (indeed, it is the progenitor of that category): it had granular work, meaning that Linus Torvalds welcomed both large and small code contributions to the project, and the work was modular, which meant that no contributors needed necessarily to wait for other contributors to complete their work before submitting their own. The project also had low costs of fixation, in that its publication costs were simply the cost of typing on a computer. The project would have low costs of transmission, too, since it involved sending code over an Internet connection. There would be an environment of public information, since all discourse participants would have access to the same code, and no one member would enjoy any advantage by holding back code from any other member—in fact, there would be a distinct disadvantage to doing so, since that would impede verification of the submission's usefulness. The last category of CBPP, successful low-cost integration, is the one upon which all success or failure turns. Many projects or discourses can meet all of the above requirements, but cannot achieve low-cost integration. Linux achieves low-cost integration through the nature of the project (unlike text for human consumption, computer code can be readily tested to see if it works) and its deep pool of contributors.

The Linux CBPP project owes much of its success to its ability—intended or not—to implement the fundamentals of epistemic rhetoric. In Linux, the work product is rhetorically situated between multiple parties. To make a direct analogy to the rhetorical epistemic network, it is not too much to suggest that indeed truth itself is situated as a rhetorical object between multiple participants. Now consider that, for Linux development, "truth" is defined quite narrowly: one can make all kinds of claims on open-source discussion boards such as Slashdot about the nature of the open source community, but the best way to evaluate a "truth claim" in this code-writing community is to test whether or not the code works. While discussions about the value of a code contribution can affect its integration, the Linux community has the advantage of first asking whether the contribution works before considering whether it is relevant. These gatekeepers are essential, because the Linux community is an example of a very robust, energetic, and vast network of epistemic rhetoric: each of the network nodes can contribute to the code, and can weigh in on the value of the code. Whenever there are a great number of nodes in a network, there is a great demand for integrating the contributions.

What is the most direct path, then, to integrating the multiple contributions of a robust epistemic network? A clearly defined purpose for the network, or, a clearly defined topic is essential for efficient integration. The history of the concept of "topic" in rhetoric is rich. It ranges from Aristotle's *topoi*, as an invention aid, to Bolter's electronic notion of "topographic" writing. Bolter explains that "a text as network may have no univocal sense. It can remain a multiplicity without the imposition of a principle of domination. In place of hierarchy, we have a writing space that is not only topical; we might even call it 'topographic.' The word 'topography' originally meant a written description of a place, such as an ancient geographer might give. Only later did the word come to refer to mapping or charting—that is, to a visual and mathematical rather than verbal description. Electronic writing can be both a visual and verbal description. It is not the writing of a place, but rather writing with places as spatially realized topics" (2001, 36).

Bolter's notion of topographic writing is helpful if we wish to understand how "topic" works within a CBPP system. We may start with more of a conventional sense of the term—a category for arranging ideas—but when one begins to see topicality as the means for judging whether or not CBPP contributions are relevant to the project, then Bolter's more interconnected definition of "topography" is more accurate. CBPP systems rely on clearly defined topics to assess the relevancy of contributions, and since off-topic contributions would distort the meaning of the overall project, all contributions are reviewed for how they will affect the overall project—or, in terms of place, how the arrival of new content will affect the remaining pages. If a network identifies a clearly defined topic, it is possible to develop any number of measures for integrating contributions, including evaluations of substance, style, format, length, efficacy, and so on. But while the epistemic network assures a great richness, since its truth is defined through the interaction among contributing nodes, it is another school of transactional rhetoric that provides the clearest and most practical consideration of how to develop clear measures for the integration of contributions.

The Role of Classical Rhetoric in a CBPP Network

Successful CBPP integration is fed by the structure of classical rhetoric and how it positions truth claims. The debate between Plato and Aristotle about the role of rhetoric creates a firm divide between science and art, or what is knowable through independent verification and what is knowable through the senses. In *The Rhetorical Tradition*, Patricia Bizzell and Bruce Herzberg write that "for Plato, false rhetoric is precisely that [which] relies on *kairos* or the situation in order to determine provisional truth or probably knowledge. Plato faults the Sophists for not using rhetoric to try to discover absolute truth" (2001, 28). For Aristotle, however, rhetoric plays no role in absolute truth, but, "that does not mean that rhetoric is useless to Aristotle—far from it. . . . Aristotle values rhetoric as an aid to reaching agreement on questions of value or preference that demand immediate action in everyday life" (31). Berlin summarizes the divide this way: "Science and logic are outside the rhetorical realm since both are concerned with the indisputable, with certainties that do not ordinarily lead to disagreement. The truths of rhetoric, on the other hand, are by their very nature uncertain, open to debate, contingent, probable. They deal not just with the empirical or rational analysis of experience, but with the emotional, aesthetic, and ethical—in other words, with the total range of human behavior" (1987, 15). For CBPP, this distinction between what truth is verifiable and which truths are contingent is pivotal for evaluating user contributions.

Recall Benkler's definition of low-cost integration as the ability of the CBPP project, or rhetorical discourse community, to weed out inadequate or off-topic contributions. He writes that "a successful peer production enterprise must have low-cost integration, which includes both quality control over the modules and a mechanism for integrating the contributions into the finished product" (379). In the realm of a coding CBPP project such as Linux, that would mean the project would have the ability to verify each piece of code's functionality, and the ability to integrate multiple contributions into a meaningful whole. When presented by Benkler, this seems to be a clear-cut task—verify that the code works and that the code is needed.

In practice, these are two very challenging and complex tasks, a reality that is clarified by the distinction in ancient rhetoric between the business of science and the business of rhetoric. Distinguishing between computer code that works and code that does not work should be fairly easy: you load it up on a machine and test it. But what if that code does indeed work as the author intended it to do, but accomplishes a function that is not part of the perceived goal of the overall project? Here again is the famous distinction between science and rhetoric: testing whether or not the code contribution works is the business of science—a truth claim which is easily verified or discredited. Testing whether or not the code contribution is valuable? This is the business of rhetoric. The transactional network is structured to handle both types of truth claims. Whether integrating content into the CBPP network is cheap and easy or nebulous and tedious, the rhetorical principle of defining truth through the conversation among nodes in the network is stable and verifiable.

In fact, the very task of addressing what is and what is not a valuable—as opposed to a valid—contribution in CBPP is the very discussion that should be taking place in academic classrooms, especially in terms of student contributions to established academic disciplines. To defend a challenge from the CBPP system as to the value of a particular contribution is an inherently rich composition task. It requires that the contributor relate the worth of the contribution to the discourse community in terms of that community's stated goals. In other words, topics play a more prominent role in the CBPP composition classroom. To avoid a situation in the electronic, epistemic, CBPP writing network where all truth is regarded as relative, student writers need to be focused on the role of topics as defined goals for network projects. In a social network such as MySpace, a student writer might be able to offer unqualified opinions about any number of subjects, but within professional networks such as an open-source software development project, contributions have to be verified to become valuable to the group. In essence, CBPP topics define the discourse community: the methods within each CBPP community for verifying the accuracy and relevance of contributions are a statement of its ethos, or an epistemic reflection of what it believes to be possible and practical act within the knowledge community. But this is no different from what we ask student writers to accomplish when we attempt to prepare them to write in different knowledge communities today through the practices of Writing Across the Curriculum initiatives or various professional documentation standards. The CBPP composition experience thrusts upon writers the full weight of making meaning for a discourse community and ultimately calls upon them to employ sound techniques of persuasion to defend their contributions.

But while classical rhetoric's distinction between scientific claims and rhetorical claims is helpful in terms of identifying CBPP contributions, it is less pragmatic in terms of resolving these claims. A CBPP project cannot simply decide whether or not to retain a submission based upon validity. It must make the more relative judgment of how the contribution is or is not valuable. This is where the fundamentals of epistemic rhetoric offer a much broader perspective. In epistemic rhetoric, knowledge itself is a rhetorical construct. Since epistemic rhetoric assumes that language itself is part of the meaning-making process and that truth is not external to this process, it provides instruction for writers in CBPP who wish to defend the worth of their challenged contributions.

The defense of last resort for a challenged contribution is what is known in the hacking community as "forking." Forking describes what happens when some contributors take the code base and create a new project with different goals. Many open source developers view forking as a group failure, assuming that if the mother project had been able to accommodate the interests of all contributors through compromise, then it would have remained a stronger project. But epistemic rhetoric teaches us that a stable consensus within large discourse communities is simply impossible. If the community itself is defined by diverse participants, then the size of the community is the direct inverse of its chance for consensus. This has certainly been borne out in the history of Linux developments; all of the many Linux distributions/distros (Fedora, Debian, SUSE, etc.) have been the result of forking, or the rejection of contributions on the grounds of lack of value, rather than lack of validity. The relationship back to rhetoric, then, is that while classical rhetoric is valuable in pointing up the distinction between what is a conflict of opinion and what is a conflict of fact, epistemic rhetoric acknowledges that these conflicts are inherent within the system. Thus, the perspective of classical rhetoric is useful in terms of defining CBPP conflicts over what constitutes a relevant or accurate contribution. If, however, a contribution is rejected on either grounds, the perspective of epistemic rhetoric means that perhaps the potential CBPP contribution merely has not yet found the correct CBPP project.

Conflict resolution within CBPP systems is a new field of inquiry. Many who have written in Wikipedia or have had experience contributing to open-source software projects can attest to the truth that as long as one offers content in a CBPP system, it is only a matter of time before that content is questioned. This questioning should be viewed as part of the integration process and is actually a measure of the activity and health of any particular CBPP system. The major difference, however, between transactional rhetoric's approach and the conflict resolution procedures of many existing CBPP projects is the practical need for a project to reach some type of consensus in order to advance the overall state of the project. A rhetorical theory need not predict how discourse participants will behave in terms of coming to consensus; in practice, however, the health and vitality of a discourse community might very well depend on how it resolves disputes. The very qualities of epistemic rhetoric that ensure rich conversation and a tolerance for multiple perspectives also ensure a great divergence among writers and a difficulty in reaching consensus. Ultimately, guidance for dispute resolution in a CBPP project comes from a clearly defined topic for the entire project, for that topic, or purpose, is the ultimate authority for determining which contributions are relevant and which are not. Contributors can refer only to the purpose of the CBPP system to gauge the relevance of any particular contribution. Epistemic rhetoric makes no such demands on contributions; it just seeks to advance conversation by defining multiple perspectives and ensuring that truth remains suspended among participants holding those perspectives.

In this manner, it is possible to view CBPP as a direct extension of epistemic rhetorical theory, moving from simply ensuring that truth exists in suspension among multiple discourse participants to a more finely tuned position of deciding whether a statement is on topic and then, if so, credible. Since rhetorical theory drives composition theory, this is an important distinction: student writers verifying the factual accuracy of statements by other student writers has not normally been part of the composition classroom. With CBPP systems, however, it is essential to consider whether an utterance is on topic and credible. If this is a valuable problem from the standpoint of instruction—if we can assume that writers will need the skills of assessing the relevance and accuracy of content within a CBPP system as a rhetorical task—then the experience of writing within a CBPP system is an asset for the composition classroom for yet another reason. Composition classrooms have long employed peer-response mechanisms for the purpose of improving authors' texts through their responders' prompts, and also for the purpose of broadening the responders' own work through greater exposure to how other writers in the classroom are responding to writing challenges. But we have rarely, if ever, asked student writers to share the role of evaluating the relevance and accuracy of other students' texts for inclusion in a CBPP system.

Benkler defines the criteria for submissions within CBPP as "relevance" and "accreditation" (2002, 390–96). While giving voice to detractors of CBPP systems, Benkler writes, "You might say that many distributed individuals can produce content, but that it is gobbledygook. Who in their right mind wants to get answers to legal questions from a fifteen-year-old child who learned the answers watching Court TV? The question then becomes whether relevance and accreditation of initial utterances of information itself can be produced on a peer production model. The answer is that it can" (390–91). Benkler continues to elucidate several models of successful low-cost integration, or examples of Internet sites of collaboration where contributors commingle the roles of contribution and evaluation. One of the most famous of these models is Slashdot.

Slashdot as a Robust Epistemic Network

Slashdot.org is a large website in almost every sense of the term "large." Ostensibly, the focus of the site is open-source software. In reality, its users are people with a shared interest in open-source software and a higher than average interest in Internet technology, culture, theory, and law. Most important, however, is the fact that Slashdot users write a lot, and their enthusiasm for self-expression translates into a site with a great deal of energy. The site model operates with users submitting news stories, usually as seen on other sites, to the editors of Slashdot. If the editors feel that a story will be of interest to Slashdot readers, then they assign it a category, write a brief description, and post it at Slashdot with a link back to the source site. Slashdot readers are then able to write their own comments to the story onto the Slashdot site. Recently, Slashdot's influence has been challenged by a similar site, *digg.com*, that has the important distinction of having no editorial board—news stories are submitted by users into a pool, and after they accumulate enough votes, or "diggs," they are advanced to the front page. Even more complex is *newsvine.com*, which not only allows users to vote or "seed stories onto the vine" but also offers them the ability to tag content and post blogs, complete with monetary compensation. However, Slashdot was the first site to make a real breakthrough in terms of assessing content submissions and user submissions for accuracy and relevance to the site.

When a reader posts comments to Slashdot, those comments are ranked by other readers on a scale from –1 to 5. This process is called "moderation" or "modding" (see the complete Slashdot moderation FAQ at *slashdot.org/faq/com-mod.shtml*). Slashdot readers who participate in the discussion board by logging in and posting comments that are themselves modded as valuable are from time to time offered "points." Each point is in effect the ability to mod another user's comment. Points disappear if not used in a certain amount of time. Further, Slashdot assigns each user a "karma" score ranging from "Terrible" (–1) to "Excellent" (5). Karma value is intended to reflect how well one participates within the Slashdot discussion, and it is based on how often one posts comments, how valuable those comments are to the community—as determined through the moderation system—and whether or not one contributes story submissions. Karma also determines the initial mod value of one's comments. For instance, if you have a high karma value as a logged-in user, your comments will start with a mod score of 1 or higher, whereas if you post comments without logging in or have a poor karma score, your comments will start at zero or lower.

What is to keep readers from abusing their power to score other comments? Why, for instance, would a user not simply mod down unpopular opinions or the comments of posters whom they dislike? Slashdot features a meta-moderation system. From time to time, valued users are given the ability to review other users' moderation by assessing the ratings assigned to comments. If the system finds that a user consistently mods (marks a comment) too far up or too far down, then it can rank the very rating of that user's rating, and that user will be given fewer mod points in the future. Thus, Slashdot creates a robust peer-review system that composition teachers must envy in terms of its breadth and depth of commenting (it is not uncommon for stories to generate more than 1,000 remarks), its ability to clearly assign value to comments (thereby encouraging submission of even more valuable comments and discouraging off-topic and less valuable comments), and its ability to create a quantifiable ethos amongst participants, as well as its ability to encourage even more dialogue. Slashdot offers a model for what CBPP could look like as applied to the composition classroom if enough participation could be created. Slashdot solves the problem of audience contact for the firm model composition classroom: as a robust CBPP network, the Slashdot model reduces transaction costs by facilitating immediate and voluminous audience response to writers' words, rather than asking its equivalent of a writing instructor to conjure those responses. Similarly, the Slashdot model dramatically lowers invention costs: work is granular and largely modular, so writers are free to comment as much or as little as they wish on the topic of their choosing. The *digg.com* model reduces invention costs further still since it distributes across the network the job of determining which story submissions to publish.

While comments are assigned a number to indicate their value, they also feature text descriptions that give a glimmer of insight into what the Slashdot discourse community finds valuable. Good adjectives are "Informative" or "Interesting," while negative adjectives include "Flamebait," "Troll," or "Offtopic." Flamebaiting refers to the practice of writing incendiary comments from a polemical point of view, with the purpose of luring people into emotional responses of outrage rather than entering into honest discourse. A Slashdot comment assigned the label of "Troll" is considered to be annoying. "Offtopic" is self-explanatory. Quantifying the discourse community's opinion about contributions allows readers several options, not the least of which is the ability to browse comments with a set threshold. Readers might want only to see the comments deemed as the best by the Slashdot readers. If so, that reader can set the comment viewing through to the level of "5" and only view comments that other readers rated as the highest.

From the standpoint of CBPP, then, Slashdot does an admirable job of distributing back to its readers the essential functions of deciding which contributions to the project are on-topic and which are not relevant. In addition to solving the relevance problem, Slashdot has also accomplished much in the way of solving the accreditation problem through the process of ranking not only comments but also commenters. Thus, on a rhetorical level, Slashdot participants have a quantifiable ethos that demonstrably affects their contributions. Perhaps even more remarkable is the manner in which Slashdot has been able to take a very elusive concept—a perpetually defined value of the contributor in terms of content submitted a CBPP system—and readily apply it to CBPP contributions. Slashdot serves as an excellent example of epistemic rhetoric as applied to a CBPP network: participants in the discourse community perpetually determine which statements are true and accurate—for them—by perpetually discussing them. The text and its truth are always external to the participants, and always in the process of being determined through the input of discourse.

The fact that truth is continually defined at Slashdot makes it an epistemic network, but it is a transactional network as well. Transaction costs, or the impediments of the writer to reach an audience, must first be reduced before the Slashdot model works. In evaluating transaction costs within the Slashdot board, however, it is worth considering that the article that triggers responses is almost never written by any of the contributors. It is almost always written by an outsider. Therefore, even though there has never been any lack of outspokenness on the board, the author is not part of the discussion, and the text of the Slashdot discourse network, rather than being an extension of an original submission, consists of the comments of the thousands of Slashdot users. Therefore, if the potential for negative reaction of the author to comments perhaps raises transaction costs by discouraging comments, such as it often does in composition classrooms when peer reviewers express anxiety about offending another student writer, the Slashdot model reduces that potential by focusing comments on a third-party article. As these comments become the text of the epistemic network, they are perfectly conditioned as CBPP particles: Slashdot comments are modular (they are almost always nonsequential as they all follow the initial article); they are granular (some of the most popular remarks are pithy one-liners); they exist within a network where all knowledge is assumed to be public (even though conspiracy theorists thrive within Slashdot); and the cost of integrating them is low.

Slashdot's low transaction costs and robust peer-response interactions invite us to interrogate the nature of utterances as transactions in their fullest sense, both economically and rhetorically. No cash changes hands within Slashdot, yet writers are compensated for their contributions. The currency of Slashdot is measurable in terms of both increased speaker ethos and speaker volume; that is, the transactions in Slashdot perpetuate the rhetorical values of the discourse community. As we have already reviewed in the examination of Slashdot's modding system, if you contribute often to the discussion, then you are "paid" with a quantifiable ethos (your comments begin with a more valuable score), and you have the ability to score other's remarks. Further, since your remarks are scored more highly, then you exercise increased volume, for more readers are likely to see your comments—since some readers filter comments to see only the ones with high ratings.

Thus, while Slashdot remains an inherently epistemic network with lowered transaction costs, it pushes teachers of writing to think of how it furthers the concept of a transaction within strictly rhetorical terms. Earlier, we observed that in a rhetorical sense, transaction costs were the impediments that a speaker overcame in order to reach his or her audience. The Slashdot model extends this concept of communication with the audience as a transaction by allowing the network to compensate the speaker, if his or her message is both valuable and on-topic to the network, with greater rhetorical stature. Thus, the CBPP network can establish rhetorical credibility as a currency: when a Slashdot contributor adds valuable content, then he or she is compensated with greater credibility and volume. Similarly, if the speaker's utterances are not as valuable to the network as a whole, then that speaker suffers lower credibility through the form of lower karma and fewer mod points. Thus, speakers whose content is consistently valued find that their transaction costs are lowered over time, whereas speakers who are off-topic or offer less insight are further distanced from their audience.

A great flexibility for this particular system is that the standard of truth is constantly in play. Since the comment-modding process seeks the opinions of a great number of readers dispersed over a vast network, there is a bedrock of consistency in the reaction to utterances. Ultimately, however, the judgment of what constitutes truth in this epistemic network is left up to judgment, and even though it is a nearly instantaneous response of a large majority, it is still susceptible to the swings and fallacies of popular opinion. It is important to note, however, that once opinion is as broadly dispersed and as instantaneous as a CBPP network can make it, it takes on perhaps some more durable qualities associated with polling. But in the end, the mod system on Slashdot asks readers to rank opinion. This is qualitatively different from the CBPP network of scientific endeavors, where readers and network participants are asked to attempt to duplicate the speaker's truth to either solidify or refute his or her claims. Thus the flexibility of truth claims within an epistemic network such as Slashdot has both strengths and limitations.

If the Slashdot network fulfills all the requirements of CBPP and is an epistemic network demonstrating low transaction costs, can it stand as a prototype for importing CBPP into the composition classroom? Certainly the question invites a more thorough consideration of transactional behaviors within this particular epistemic network. Any attempt to use the Slashdot model in the composition classroom would have to acknowledge at least four essential limitations: scale, contributions, moderation, and currency. The Slashdot epistemic network needs a particular critical mass in order to ensure its dynamic richness. While acquiring software is not a problem (the Slashdot code and many more appropriate substitutes are all open-source), building an environment that would assure that postings are read and commented upon is a much more difficult problem: a comment that is rated a "5—Informative" level in a network of twenty-five first-year composition users is a substantially different judgment than one from a network of more than 100,000 users. Additionally, composition classrooms need to promote students' writing, and the Slashdot model is built around discoursing in reaction to another's writing. The Slashdot process could be adopted to posting an assigned class reading, asking student writers to comment on that reading, and allowing them to mod each other's comments. Modding presents the greater challenge, but it is the heart of the network. Student writers would need a robust network to ensure honest reactions to each other's comments, free of quid pro quo. Establishing an epistemic Slashdot type of network that transcended institutional boundarie would solve the problems of size, by ensuring that enough student writers could participate to generate substantial comments, as well as reducing the chance of establishing a payback system for commentaries. Yet it is the very risk of inappropriate payment by writers for positive comments on their texts that reveals perhaps the most important concern to examine in importing a Slashdot epistemic network into classrooms: currency. How are writers rewarded for good writing?

Currency

The currency of the college composition classroom is the grade earned by the student for acquiring and demonstrating composition skills. There is no disputing this truth, and there is no simple method to harness its impact for pedagogical objectives. Any attempt to import CBPP into the writing classroom must first acknowledge how the current firm model of composition encourages certain behaviors while discouraging others through the currency of course grades. Just like the firm manager, the composition instructor rewards those who produce results that, as discussed in Chapter 1, the instructor deems as writing that a market would find valuable. The most immediate problem facing any teacher who would seek to import a CBPP network is how to integrate that network into the existing reward structure.

Further complicating the currency problem is the fact that much CBPP work also dissolves the traditional roles of author and reader, asking students to work in collaboration with other writing students or people in the CBPP network who are not enrolled in the class, or both. Clearly, the instructor has no control over other actors in the CBPP network. An assignment such as writing for a Wikipedia page challenges traditional assessment models, since the student has no authorial control over his or her work: anyone is free to delete the work or—even more challenging for the instructor—to modify sentences within it word for word. It is possible for the writing instructor to track exactly what the student contributed, but with the limitations of current technology, it is quite a forensic exercise to ascertain its value and how it added value to the overall project. In the current firm composition model, all writing is the sole property of the individual student, submitted to the instructor as his or her own creation. Though that model has numerous flaws, it excels in offering clarity for a reward structure. It is simple to determine who wrote what and who receives what grade for it. Indeed, the sole authorship model stands as a major obstacle for the adoption of CBPP for the composition teachers themselves—the discipline of English has clung to the sole authorship model for years in spite of the developments of electronic media, the success of the science model of joint authorship attribution, and the complications of critical theory itself toward the very possibility of sole authorship. A response for the currency problem in the composition classroom, however, is fairly straightforward when compared to the entrenched interests that deter change in the professional organizations of its teachers.

The approach to integrating CBPP into the composition classroom and successfully answering the compensation question should be developed along two lines: principles and practices. When attempting to determine how we value writing conducted, essentially, entirely outside the classroom on a CBPP network such as Wikipedia, instructors must look to the principles of composition instruction—as informed by rhetorical theory—to guide assessment and ward off panic. Likewise, in practice, electronic portfolios allow student writers to review and package many discrete writing "bits"—granularized work—into an intelligent and cohesive whole. While CBPP dissolves the role of authorship and makes composition work difficult to attribute to a particular student for the sake of rewards, the portfolio not only allows the student to reassemble the work in a meaningful narrative for presentation to audiences outside the composition classroom but the reflective practices it occasions also allows student writers to apply critical thinking skills in assessing their own work as a meta-reinforcement of the overall goals of the composition classroom.

While portfolio practices can assist with assessment problems created by the granularity and modularity of CBPP writing assignments, it is transaction theory that again suggests new opportunities for assessing writing produced in the CBPP classroom. Economic transaction cost theory instructs us that CBPP offers lower transaction costs by placing the writer in closer proximity with the reader. If we fundamentally alter the teaching arrangement in the composition classroom by replacing the firm model with a CBPP network, then we have also fundamentally altered the flow of academic currency. If student writers have faster and more immediate access to their audiences, then there is less need for an instructor to replicate the audience's reaction to the student's text. Instead, the writing instructor can now assign at least a portion of the currency—the process of acknowledging effective writing—directly to the student's audience. Any number of schemes are imaginable in a CBPP network, where audience feedback can play a direct and quantifiable role in assessing the qualities of student writing. This need not mean that the instructor surrender all authority in assigning grades. Instead of acting as the sole source for assessment, however, the instructor of the CBPP writing classroom can focus on assisting the writer to assess for himself or herself audience feedback and make changes in the text to improve its reach. This reconceptualization of assessment and academic currency will no doubt give some readers pause. However, if we accept the premise of epistemic rhetoric that truth is made in a dialogue between writer and reader and reject the objectivist and subjectivist notions that it is held exclusively by either party, then assigning the audience a greater role in assessing the effectiveness of the student writer's prose is a logical development. This does not mean that the writing instructor abdicates the responsibilities of assessment. Instead, increasing the role of the audience through indirect assessment of student writing emphasizes the instructor's role in training the writer to interpret audience feedback accurately and to make textual adjustments.

Transaction Costs, Audience Proximity, and Invention Costs

While the economic model provides witness to the performance of lowered transaction costs between writer and audience in CBPP, one still must investigate how it affects what might be termed the writer's invention costs, or the difficulties of conceiving a writing project or topic. Economic theory, especially firm theory, does anticipate the costs of coordinating input from various contributors, but not specifically the costs incurred when we brainstorm material for writing. In terms of transactional rhetoric, invention costs are lower in CBPP because of the writer's increased proximity to the audience or the text. Just as the closer proximity to audience lowers the transaction costs of writing in CBPP, so too does that nearness lower the invention costs as the writer benefits from seeing the existing text, acknowledging the *kairos* of a particular CBPP contribution, inventorying his or her own creativity, and envisioning a fit between his or her creative output into the existing text. To examine the claim that being closer to audience and text aids the creation of content in CBPP, it is worth looking more closely at the most popular tools for describing audience in contemporary composition theory.

Contemporary composition theory analysis of audience has been profoundly influenced by the thinking of Lisa Ede and Andrea Lunsford, particularly in their seminal article "Audience Addressed/Audience In-voked: The Role of Audience in Composition Theory and Pedagogy" (1984). Ede and Lunsford offer the terms "audience addressed" and "au-dience invoked" to describe a split between the ways writers interact with their audiences and, in turn, the manner in which audiences impact their writers. Though the distinction is not new (Ede and Lunsford credit Henry W. Johnstone Jr. and Chaim Perelman), what these authors bring to the conceptualization is a distinct phrasing of two extremes in audi-ence awareness and a memorable way to navigate between them. For Ede and Lunsford, those who "envision audience as addressed emphasize the concrete reality of the writer's audience; they also share the assumption that knowledge of this audience's attitudes, beliefs, and expectations is not only possible (via observation and analysis) but essential" (321), In contrast to "those who envision audience as invoked stress that the au-dience of a written discourse is a construction of the writer" (325). For Ede and Lunsford, these two extreme caricatures of audience both get it wrong; they argue that each side "has failed to adequately recognize 1) the fluid, dynamic character of rhetorical situations; and 2) the inte-grated, interdependent nature of reading and writing" (321).

At first, it would seem that CBPP would favor the idea of an audi-ence addressed, since it pulls the audience much closer to the writer, of-ten creating the situation of CBPP co-authors working on the same text. But because CBPP reduces transaction costs between writers and audi-ences, it also brings forth the very condition that Ede and Lunsford an-ticipated when they spoke of the "fluid, dynamic character of rhetorical situations." Writers no longer need to invoke audiences, since the mecha-nism of electronic communication within a healthy and dynamic CBPP environment allows for varied and instant responses. Writers are also not forced to consider only the audience addressed since they can choose when and where to submit text within the CBPP network, releasing as much or as little text as they are prepared to reveal (granularity) and on a schedule that suits their needs (modularity). The CBPP dynamic ulti-mately reduces the distance between author and audience, since members of the audience all share the same potential for contributing text. CBPP does not erase the identity of authorship by obfuscating identity through collaboration. Instead, CBPP fundamentally transforms identity by clari-fying the audience's access to the text. When the roles of author and audience become interchangeable and fluctuate rapidly, then control over a text requires a consensus between authors and audience. CBPP is not only a more "fluid, dynamic" rhetorical situation than Ede and Lunsford could have anticipated in 1984, but it is also a full manifestation of what they called "the integrated, interdependent nature of reading and writing" (321).

In describing this middle ground, Ede and Lunsford write that "the most complete understanding of audience thus involves a synthesis of the perspectives we have termed audience addressed, with its focus on the reader, and audience invoked, with its focus on the writer" (332). To visualize this environment, the authors offer an illustration of "the concept of audience." The figure is a wheel, with the writer at the hub and spokes running outward to invoked audience roles—"self, friend, colleague, critic, mass audience, future audience, past audience, anomalous audience"—and addressed-audience roles—"future audience, mass audience, critic, colleague, friend, self" (331). Surely the fundamental placement of writers in a CBPP environment—with little impediment to two-way communication between people with an equal chance to read, contribute, or alter text—best represents the highest manifestation of this invigorated composing environment. Ede and Lunsford write about the composition of their own essay to illustrate their point that the best model of the composing environment represents input and edits not only between themselves as co-authors but also between several readers from whom they sought input during the composition of the article.

Because CBPP reduces the transaction costs between author and audience, it might be tempting to think that the CBPP environment favors audience addressed over audience invoked. After all, in CBPP the author need not wait to seek out the audience addressed; they too are contributing to the same project, most likely editing the same text the author is offering. But even though the CBPP writing environment raises the profile of the audience addressed, the audience invoked still retains its invaluable place in the writer's consciousness. This role is invigorated by the immediacy of the addressed audience, and as long as other contributors in the CBPP system do not actually invade the author's consciousness, there will always be a need for audience invoked. The difference is that, within the CBPP environment, the potential gap between audience addressed and audience invoked is considerably diminished. Ede and

Lunsford seemingly call for this very environment when they offer that "a fully elaborated view of audience, then, must balance the creativity of the writer with the different, but equally important, creativity of the reader" (334).

In citing the immediacy of audience contact in CBPP as a method of invigorating the author's relationship to the audience, some caution is needed. Not all theorists would contend that quick and easy access to the audience is beneficial to the composition process. Peter Elbow sides with other expressivists such as Donald Murray when he advises caution with audience contact in "Closing My Eyes as I Speak: An Argument for Ignoring Audience." Elbow writes that "putting audience out of mind is of course a traditional practice: serious writers have long used private journals for early explorations of feeling, thinking, or language. But many writing teachers seem to think that students can get along without the private writing serious writers find so crucial—or even that students will benefit from keeping their audience in mind for the whole time. Things often don't work out that way" (2000, 337). Elbow then cites examples where student writers get into trouble and consistently produce poor results because of a proximity to audience. He compares writing to acting, implying that, like good acting, good writing happens only when the actor is able to ignore the audience—to squelch stage fright—and become rapt in the content of his or her performance. He implies that reading is akin to the acting performance—that the writer/actor has been transported to a place far away, and that we, too, the reader/audience, wish to join her. But even though Elbow indulges in some romantic language to make his points, it is the very structure of his argument that undercuts the furthest claims of his essay.

Elbow breaks his claims for ignoring audience into two stages, the "limited" and the "more ambitious." This calls to mind his helpful techniques of breaking writing projects into stages, developed in *Writing Without Teachers* and elsewhere. Elbow has argued, rather convincingly, for writing strategies that fully separate the roles of creator and editor (1998, 5–7). In so many words, he contends that firewalling the creator off from the editor allows for creativity and volume in prose; correspondingly, the editor has a better chance of seeing the form of text and "hearing" how the text sounds for audiences when freed from the task of creating text. Elbow's argument to ignore the audience is no different. The lesson for those of us who wish to integrate CBPP into the composition classroom is that writers will need a safe place to develop text before placing it before an audience or sharing it with co-editors. The need for such an incubation period grows, in fact, when students shift from writing only to classmates and instructors to the audience-empowered environment of CBPP. Before student writers can produce text and open it up for co-editing, they need to have a chance to hear their own words. Writing in a CBPP environment can be consistent with this practice—there is no need to have student projects start on the wiki. As Elbow states, "Ignoring audience can lead to worse drafts but better revisions" (2000, 338). In fact, writing in a CBPP system can accelerate creativity because it extends the writer's inward focus from the typical composition classroom experience of invention for an assigned topic to a self-examination of his or her creative impulses, expertise, and interests for topic selection. Elbow's bifurcation of the creative and editorial processes is useful to CBPP composition processes because the act of creation is extended from invention to topic selection.

CBPP Merges Solitary and Collaborative Writing Processes

When one mentions the concept of collaborative learning in composition circles, the work of Kenneth Bruffee is almost always cited. *Collaborative Learning* is a touchstone work for teachers of writing who are interested in collaborative learning strategies. In setting up the topic of the book, Bruffee begins with a personal anecdote about his experience as a new and overwhelmed writing program administrator at Brooklyn College during the institution's first year of open admission (1999, 3–7). To cope with the flood of students in the hallways, Bruffee writes that he sought the company of other WPAs at sister institutions, figuring that they might have answers for his administrative problems. When he set up their initial meeting, he quickly learned that these fellow administrators did not have the authoritative answer for his problem—as a consequence, however, they formed a regularly-meeting support group for people seeking answers for similar problems. By coming together and working collaboratively on the problem of how best to handle the demands of numerous students who had not received the K–12 training needed for college, they formed a prototype of the very answer they were seeking.

Most of their students were from a socioeconomic background that infrequently intersected with college graduates. Bruffee identifies the process of moving from one culture to another as key to their ability to survive and learn; for the students, this process of acculturation was emotional and psychological as well as intellectual, as the students were often encountering the culture of the academy for the first time. In this educational transformation, Bruffee found a common strategy for all learning processes, stating broadly that people "reacculturate themselves by working together. That is, there is a way to sever, weaken, or renegotiate our ties to one or more of the communities we belong to and at the same time gain membership in another community. We can do that if, and it seems in most cases only if, we work collaboratively. What we have to do, it appears, is to organize or join a temporary support or transition group on the way to our goal, as we undergo the trials of changing allegiance from one community to another" (7–8).

Thus, Bruffee sees forming these support groups for students in the process of moving to an academic community as an approach to successful college learning. In reference to his own support group of beleaguered administrators, Bruffee describes them also as knowledge seekers. Unlike their acculturating students, they were experienced professional academics who were quite comfortable gathering knowledge through traditional research. However, they were similar to their students in that the community of learners dramatically affected how they came to value what they read. Bruffee observes, "Although we learned a lot from what we read, we learned a lot more from what we said to one another about what we read. . . . In the process we became a new community. It was a knowledge community in which members talked about college and university education as quintessentially reacculturative and talked about reacculturation as quintessentially collaborative" (9). Bruffee argues then that the process of learning is essentially the same for all of us, whether or not we are experienced academics: All learning is the process of moving from one knowledge group to another. In this way, we can envision that engaging in scholarship and traditional library research is actually the process of engaging in conversation with various knowledge communities scattered across time and organized by topic.

Bruffee's analysis of engaging in learning communities clearly antici-pates the act of writing in CBPP. When writing in an extended CBPP system, one encounters the same dynamic of entering a new knowl-edge community, stepping from a traditional learning community into an electronic one. Instead of the speakers being located in the library, however, they are scattered across a global network, with participants able to respond to almost immediately to new developments. For ex-ample, in October 2003, I was trying to explain to my colleague Sam that Wikipedia was an online encyclopedia that anyone could edit. Sam could not believe that the content would be either readable or re-motely accurate, so we opened Wikipedia on his computer terminal and I asked him to look up any topic he could possibly imagine. He was startled. "Any topic?" he asked. "Any topic," I answered. Sam en-tered "professional wrestling," and up came a comprehensive encyclo-pedia entry with definitions, history, discussion of rules, themes, char-acters, cultural impact, and sources. The entry was so credible, in fact, that Sam had a difficult time accepting that anyone could edit it at any time. After going back and forth on this concept several times, I decided that the only way to illustrate this to him was to insist that he alter the entry himself. He typed "CAGE MATCH!!!!!!!!!!!!" into the entry, and was amazed to see that he was indeed modifying the article. Since entering gibberish (even for learning purposes) is essentially an act of vandalism, I immediately left Sam's office, walking down the hallway toward my own terminal in order to erase Sam's edit and restore the "professional wrestling" page to its previous state, but by the time I reached my com-puter—in less than five minutes—a philosophy student in Edinburgh, Scotland, had already made the appropriate change (the version of the page with Sam's edit is permanently archived at *en.wikipedia.org/w/index. php?title=Professional_wrestling&oldid=1613136*).

In terms of Bruffee's analyses, I acted as a facilitator of Sam's transi-tion from his existing knowledge community (our English department) to a new knowledge community (Wikipedia). Although Sam did not be-come a full-time participant in the new community, his orientation to Wikipedia follows Bruffee's example of a student entering into a new peer group with support of his transition from his existing knowledge group.

Adapting Bruffee's Model for the CBPP Classroom

In Bruffee's classroom model, the teacher sets the foundation for effective collaboration through the following tasks: (1) breaking students into groups of approximately five, (2) providing the students with a task, (3) reconvening students in plenary groups, and acting as a referee to negotiate consensus, (4) acting as the class's local representative of the academic community, and (5) evaluating explicitly the quality of the students' work (21). With little alteration, Bruffee's model can provide a baseline for preparing a transition of composition pedagogy from insisting on traditional instruction to accommodating CBPP in the classroom. When CBPP is applied to the composition classroom, the firm model is augmented first by moving the teacher from the position of ultimate authority (the firm manager)—dispenser of what Bruffee calls foundational knowledge—to the role of knowledge community transition facilitator. The instructor assigns groups, creates tasks, assists in the evaluation of those tasks, and assigns the ultimate grade for completion of tasks.

Bruffee's collaborative learning theory points out that CBPP in the composition classroom will require two fundamental entities in order to support students properly: support from the teacher in the role of both leader and guide, and conversation within peer groups in class. Although Bruffee does look briefly at collaboratively employing networked computers in the classroom, the second edition of *Collaborative Learning* does not anticipate the full developments of CBPP. Therefore, it is necessary to alter the praxis that Bruffee has laid out to find a richer pedagogy that will best address the needs of CBPP in the composition classroom. The CBPP component continues to allow students to self-identify tasks in the invention stage, and the lowered transaction costs of communicating with an audience allows Bruffee's newly established community to speak clearly to those students attempting to join it. This teaching strategy also relieves the instructor of the necessity of trying to speak for that new community—as dictated by the current market model of teaching (Bruffee's number four)—and allows the instructor to facilitate the transition. Additionally, the CBPP model also allows an instructor to invite the electronic network to participate in evaluation of student work, either through direct means such as comments by other CBPP contributors observed by the instructor or through quantitative data that indicates how often the CBPP system refers to the student writer's contribution.

Overall, collaborative composition theory is well-positioned for an integration with CBPP in the composition classroom. Just as CBPP also represents a successful compromise between the market model of economic production and the firm model of economic production, so too does it represent a compromise between two different composition approaches: the collaborative approach to writing and the individual approach. The two main aspects of CBPP already examined—transactional theory and network structure—provide a successful "compromise" between collaborative and individual practices in several areas, and the transactional efficiencies of CBPP place the writer in easy contact with his or her audience. That proximity to audience has the power to influence each stage of the writing process, demonstrating the general principle that CBPP encourages increased collaboration.

In essence, CBPP splits traditional views of interpreting audience reaction. CBPP keys on individuality by requiring the contributor to self-assess his or her own potential interests and skills before submitting work to a CBPP project. As mentioned earlier, this is a transactional gain in that the writer's invention occurs with a greater awareness of the audience—even if the CBPP audience is not composing jointly with the writer, the writer is more aware of the audience as participants in the epistemic network. Similarly, the writer is required to balance that freedom of topic selection against the responsibility of reaching an audience. Measures and methods of demonstrating that audience connection are similarly available to the student writer in CBPP, rather than falling to the best estimation of the writing instructor.

Introducing CBPP principles into the writing classroom reveals several limitations in commonly held pedagogical assumptions—including the limitation of asking instructors to act as audiences—and introduces new alternatives for the structure of teaching writing. Inviting electronically networked writing into the writing classroom does dramatically increase complexity and invite a great amount of potential anxiety by destabilizing the classroom discourse. But as this chapter has attempted to show, the motives for importing CBPP into the writing classroom have a solid foundation in the history of rhetorical theory and existing composition practices. CBPP's focus on reducing transaction costs and increasing audience proximity asks the instructor to relinquish authority, but rewards that move with a richer discourse that can only be experienced when instructors guide writers toward engaging varied, diverse, and professional audiences. Similarly, CBPP lowers invention costs. Since writing instructors no longer play the role of firm managers attempting to identify topics for students based on a match with their creativity, students themselves are challenged to engage their own topics. Several CBPP models, especially the discussion board Slashdot, have shown us how CBPP can help to create rich rhetorical communities.

Importing CBPP also creates potential problems when we examine the currency of composition in the traditional classroom, but there are existing models—particularly electronic portfolios—that offer proven results in addressing these challenges. Lastly, collaboration in composition theory, particularly the work of Kenneth Bruffee, is well-suited to guiding us in adding the challenges and rewards of CBPP to the writing classroom.

Given these promises, one might wonder about the particular origins of CBPP and the concept of "laziness." Chapter 5 engages exactly those questions.

5

The Origins of the Lazy Work Ethic and CBPP

What caused "laziness" to develop? Will understanding the culture of its creation assist in determining its longevity and ultimate impact in writing instruction? Understanding the origins and contexts of "laziness" and CBPP requires an understanding of its most famous iteration—Linux, the open-source operating system that started the CBPP phenomenon. And understanding Linux means, in turn, looking at the origins of Unix, the proprietary operating system of an earlier generation that provided the conceptual basis of operating systems everywhere.

The history of Unix has been recounted elsewhere, perhaps best in books such as Peter Salus's *A Quarter Century of UNIX* (1994), Glyn Moody's *Rebel Code* (2001), and Peter Wayner's *Free for All: How Linux and the Free Software Movement Undercut the High-Tech Titans* (2000). Each of these histories, however, serves a particular perspective—in some cases, that of the systems design engineer, and in other cases, that of the cultural futurist. No accounts of the history of Unix have thoroughly revealed how the fundamental components of that story showcase writing, or collaborative writing, or "laziness." With the specific foreknowledge of CBPP as a mode of economic production, the history of Unix and open source must be reevaluated and reassessed in terms of how it has contributed to the development of CBPP principles and how those contributions apply to the teaching of writing. In reevaluating the history of Unix and open-source software, this chapter will search for the origins of Benkler's concept of granularization of work and the continued practice of modularization within software development. The concepts of granularization and modularization are requirements for the development of "laziness," as without them individuals are unable to make fully independent decisions about their participation in work projects. The fundamentals of CBPP lie in the Unix story, which is part historical accident, part genius, part perseverance, and ultimately the triumph of common property rights and common sense. The story also takes rather surprising turns through gaming, fiction, collaboration, and textuality as the fundamental concepts of operating systems emerge.

What Is an Operating System?

In the contemporary era of cheap desktop computing, it is easy to forget that a computer requires a software layer known as the operating system (OS) that works underneath its visible interface and enables applications such as the word processor, Internet browser, and e-mail manager by marshalling the machine's hardware resources. One of the best and most common analogies to describe how the heart of an operating system, or its kernel, works is that of a hotel clerk. In the fictional OS hotel, there are several characters: the hotel itself serves the role of the PC, with individual hotel rooms playing the role of memory addresses, or the physical assets of the PC for running a software program. In this fictional hotel, the guests are computer programs who need to use the hotel's rooms and facilities, and the clerk plays the role of the OS kernel.

The clerk/kernel wants to make sure that the hotel's rooms are fully utilized. But she also wants to keep the guests/programs happy. Her job would be simple if each guest checked into one room for one night, and didn't want to use the kitchen, the gym, or the pool. Her job would be easier still if only one guest showed up for one room on any given night. Of course, it rarely works out that easily: her guests arrive without reservations; more guests might arrive than she has rooms for; once they are there, they might change the number of rooms the want; they might decide they want something from room service that's not on the menu; or they may clear out of a room without announcing their departure. The clerk's job is to keep the hotel running smoothly in spite of such variables. The realities of modern computing are a good deal more complicated, but the basic premise still remains: before a computer can execute an application, it needs a middle layer to communicate between the program applications and the hardware.

Ironically, operating systems have become so standardized that most computer users are scarcely aware of their existence; as Ken Thompson, a co-developer of Unix, states, "Even if you write a better operating system, nobody who actually uses computers today knows what an operating system interface is; their interface is the browser or Office" (Cooke, Urban, and Hamilton 1999). Some forty years ago, however, multiple operating systems existed to run programs on a phalanx of hardware platforms. The standard comparison of contemporary to historical computing power is often evoked by comparing a current computing environment to the computing capacity needed by NASA to send a man to the moon. That is to say, when relatively cheap desktop computers offer 512 megabytes of RAM, it is easy to forget that the Apollo guidance computer of 1969—robust enough to send man to the moon and back—worked within 30,720 bits or 3.75 kilobytes of memory. This would mean that the 512 megabytes of memory on a desktop computer have roughly enough power to launch and recover 139,810 moon shots (cf. Evans 2003). Or, to compare hardware memory to virtual memory, the average iPod of 2008 (with twenty gigabytes of memory) could power around 2,604,160 simultaneous 1969 trips to the moon.

That clichéd comparison to 1969 and space travel is key to the Unix story. In the summer of that same year, Ken Thompson, a computer programmer and Berkeley graduate, wanted to play a game on his computer at work. Since there were no such games, he decided to write it himself. If this sounds like a complicated task, it gets worse: in 1969, there was no such thing as a "personal" computer. The machine that Thompson was coding on was owned by the research institute of a very large corporation—a protected monopoly, in fact—and a partner of the military industrial complex of the Cold War United States.

Computing hardware was enormously expensive and large, so whenever a machine was purchased, its users were asked to share their access to it. This led to teams of computer users accessing the machine in 24-hour shifts. To make matters more complicated, each team authored a computer program in a high-level language, which then was reduced to an intermediate-level language (assembly code), then to the lowest-level language (machine code). Each shift of users started with a blank slate, or clear memory addresses, then loaded the machine with their program, then entered the data for the program to process. When those users' shift ended, the slate was wiped clean again, and the next user group restarted the entire cycle. Computer programs were not the sole example of recursion; their authors, too, were looping around the machine as their code was looping inside the machine.

But that is a best case scenario. Authoring good computer programs is in many respects quite similar to authoring good writing, not the least of which is that a successful program requires many drafts. Debugging takes valuable computing time, and if your shift ended before your debugging was successful, one could easily lose the progress made. This problem is more significant than the mere irritation of a few computer geeks: computer programmers and their clients were essentially attempting to solve a problem of supply and demand. Too many people needed the use of a scarce physical resource, the computer itself, and their lack of computing access was triggering inefficiencies that rippled outward. If a programmer lost debugging time, she might also lose a unique solution. Again, the parallel between writing programs and writing text succeeds at capturing the situation best: writing and revising is tough enough, but if one has to revise text between 2:00 a.m. and 5:00 a.m. under the pressure of possibly losing the revisions if the project is not completed in that three-hour framework, then the cost of the work environment is measured ultimately in terms of lost creativity and innovation. Not many minds will be maximally creative, productive, or ingenious while working under the constant threat that the entire project will disappear at any moment.

This arrangement is significant not only as a problem of political economy, but also as a formative circumstance of CBPP. Given that the scarce resource of the computing environment in the 1950s and 1960s was hardware, a great emphasis was placed on designing and manufacturing more and more powerful computers. American business management, trained by an era of successful manufacturing of material goods to win one hot war and another cold one, naturally envisioned the solution of the computing problem in terms of material production. And they were correct, initially. Before more efficient and widespread computing could take place, there would need to be a greater proliferation of machines. But the legacy of this physical problem would have a lasting twofold impact: first, an emphasis on the machine, rather than the code running on the machine, would much later lead IBM to sell the licensing rights for the operating systems on its machines to a then-obscure firm called Microsoft. This moment clearly marked the shift in most scarce computing resource from hardware to software, and the official creation of the most successful information technology monopoly in history. But more important, the scarcity of important physical computing resources would establish another enduring principle of CBPP and the last mind-set: collaboration. Most of the initial creators of Unix cut their teeth in a world of scarce computing resources, and as Steven Weber writes, this experience led in turn to a culture of collaboration amongst the rank and file programmers across the boundaries of military, academic, and business computing worlds:

> The early generation of modern computers was awkward, expensive, tricky to maintain, and not very powerful. The capabilities that we take for granted today—huge memories, fast processors, reliable and vast storage media, and, most importantly, connectivity—were hardly imaginable in 1952 when IBM put on the market the 701, its first commercial electronic computer. . . . Price aside, the hard part of owning [an early] machine was writing the instructions, or software, that told the machine what to do. . . . The engineers facing this challenge recognized the obvious next step: get everyone together who was using the machine, regardless of what company they worked for, and build [software tools] that everyone could use. . . . Everyone needed a set of basic tools, nobody could afford to build them alone, (at least not quickly enough), and efficiency dictated collaboration across corporate boundaries. (2004, 21–22)

Even after business management began to enforce a division between computer programmers and systems designers, the early atmosphere of collaboration across corporate, academic, and government boundaries prevailed in the computing community. Often, this collaboration amongst programmers was officially sanctioned by the employers, and often it was not. But in the world of scarce computing resources, collaboration was ubiquitous, and collaboration has continued as a *sine qua non* of CBPP.

Back in 1964, collaboration was also the driving force behind a project known as Multics. Before working for Bell Labs in the summer of 1969, Thompson worked on the Multics project in 1966, which was an attempt to relieve some of the problems caused by scarce computing resources. Multics was a joint project among MIT, Bell Labs, and General Electric to improve MIT's existing mainframe timesharing system, called CTSS (Compatible Time-Sharing System). The purpose of CTSS was to implement what is now termed multitasking, but for a mainframe computer system with multiple users. If the mainframe had an array of different resources, and users needed only portions of those resources at any given time, then there was a need to break up user jobs so that they kept computing resources fully-utilized. Multics was a very large project, with very ambitious goals, and very deep funding—the *Multics System Programmers' Manual* ran some 3,000 pages (Salus 1994, 29). But ultimately, Multics's size proved its undoing. Contractors were unable to meet deadlines, and by April of 1969, Bell Labs withdrew from the project, effectively terminating Multics (Salus 1994, 29). Yet, even though Multics was not the success its sponsors had hoped for, Thompson and a few others of Bell Labs' most influential programmers came away with fundamental ideas for their next project. Dennis Ritchie, another co-developer of Unix, states that "there were a lot of fundamental things we learned from Multics, [including] a tree-structured file system; a separate, identifiable program to do command interpretation [shell]; more fundamentally, the structure of files, that is, no structure, except as byte arrays, in most cases not interpreted by the operating system" (qtd. in Salus 1994, 30). These concepts—particularly the idea that "everything is a file"—would become the formative concepts of Unix.

Ken Thompson also returned from the defunct Multics project to Bell Labs to pursue that video game out of "laziness." And he was beginning to find out that the game he was designing for use on the GE-635, "Space Travel," was a very poor rendering of space flight. In Chapter 0 of *A Quarter Century of UNIX*, "Prelude to Space," Peter H. Salus narrates Thompson's unsatisfactory experience this way:

> Trapped in the plane of the ecliptic, between Mars and the asteroid belt, Ken punched a complicated maneuver into his navigational computer and glanced at the makeshift screen in front of him. <n>

[stop], <f> [front], <l> [left], <n>. Nothing. A few seconds later, he discerned barely noticeable activity. . . . Dammit, Ken muttered. Damn the folks who authorized equipment. Damn everyone in an administrative job. Damn the bean counters. It was then that he realized that this was no way to play Space Travel. The machine wasn't up to it. The software wasn't up to it. And he was going to solve the problem. (1994, 5)

It is worth pausing to reflect on the fact that Unix, the undergirding of most of the world's computing, began as a way to build a better video game. Certainly the moment can and should be celebrated by video gaming enthusiasts. But more important to this project is the understanding that gaming is closely related to "laziness" and the application of creativity. Thompson was not chastised by his employer for using computing resources to write a game; instead, Thompson's motivation for creating a game nudged him toward writing an awful lot of useful software to support it. This is not to suggest that Bell Labs knew in advance that Thompson's gaming pursuits would lead to Unix. Instead, we should consider that Unix, as the first CBPP project, was born in a pure research environment where deviation from "legitimate" work was understood to be part of the creative process. Individuals were therefore freer to engage their creativity, and ultimately that creativity reaped great rewards for the underwriting business.

At Work and Play in the Fields of Bell Labs

As a research center, Bell Labs gave a lot of latitude to its employees to determine how they would remain productive. In another article, Ritchie gives further explanation about the Bell Labs working environment where gaming played a significant role in the development of the world's most famous operating system:

Ken first did Space Travel on the GE 635. . . . It was expensive to run; a game would cost about $50. Of course it was internal "funny money."

More or less at the same time, Ken discovered the PDP-7,
which had been fitted out with a nice vector display. . . . This PDP-7
Graphics-II system was much neater than the 635's display, even if
older. The PDP-7 was a real computer, not a peripheral, albeit small
even by 1968 standards. By then, it was not used much and it was
free even by funny-money standards. So Ken moved ST to it, and
ran the game standalone. The program was written from scratch, all
in assembly language, and even including a complete floating-point
arithmetic simulator.

Also, about this time, Ken again got the urge to write his own
operating system. He had started on such a project before, but on a
much bigger machine—the GE 645 Multics machine. It didn't take
long to realize that he couldn't keep the machine.

Because Ken was now familiar with the '7 and knew he could use
it as much as he wanted, the first version of Unix was written on this
PDP-7. So ST came before Unix, but doing ST led him to a place in
which he could write the first version of Unix. (Ritchie 1998/2001)

Thus, in Ritchie's explanation, the software tools needed to run the computer were first envisioned in terms of gaming, or even more broadly
construed, fictionalization. Thompson was seeking to write an interactive
software simulation of the physics of space travel, motivated partly the
challenge of creating a performative fictional space, as well as conquering
the software and engineering challenges of creating such an environment.
Ritchie notes that "throughout his career at the Labs, Ken devoted amazing energy to games of various kinds" (Ritchie 2001). But Thompson was
interested in more than Space Travel: chess was also his passion and led
to an early game on the same PDP-7 system. There were also games such
as "Moo" (a numerical version of 21 questions), and a graphical tic-tac-
toe, but Thompson's main gaming passion was chess. The pursuit of better chess simulations would even lead Thompson to design hardware as
well as software. In summing up Thompson's passion for gaming over
the span of his career, Ritchie states that "Ken has always been a problem solver and a tool builder. He is equally excited by games, puzzles,
and technology creation, and I don't think he really distinguishes among
them" (Ritchie 2001). This perspective—that serious business and games

are on the same plane—would turn out to be central to what Pekka Himanen and Linus Torvalds would later dub "The Hacker Ethic." Computer programmers often work best when they work to achieve a specific and tangible goal. Hacking is just that—using existing resources, often in unexpected ways, to meet goals. In fact, much of computer coding is now taught in this manner: introduce a goal, then the skill, then apply the skill to meet the goal. So Thompson's contribution is not only his work on the operating system, nor only his development of the language "B," but also serving as an early example of the pragmatism of pursuing a seemingly frivolous goal—a game—and then engineering the necessary equipment to make it real.

In response to a question about his pursuit of a music collection while at work, Thompson more fully explains that "almost everything I've done is personal interest. Almost everything I've done has been supported and I'm allowed to do it, but it's always been on the edge of what's acceptable for computer science at the time. Even Unix was right on the edge of what was acceptable at Bell Labs at the time" (Cooke, Urban, and Hamilton 1999, 63).

Thompson may not have been in open rebellion against management at Bell Labs, but the fact that he at least felt as if he was "on the edge of what's acceptable" in a pure research environment serves as another precept of CBPP. Perceived transgression of expectations and boundaries joins the desire to facilitate play as a formative aspect of the CBPP creation environment. Bell Labs during the 1960s occupied a unique place within the U.S. military industrial complex. Dedicated to the pursuit of pure research, it often partnered with the government through public universities or the military. The primary difference for Bell labs, however, is the business environment: the creation and funding of these research environment labs required a massive, stable, revenue-producing base such as the legitimated monopoly that was AT&T. Certainly, AT&T management recognized that a pure research lab would pursue projects and ideas with no market potential. But eventually, work at the labs would be evaluated for its potential to create profits for AT&T. Those profits could come in the form of original research applied to the marketplace directly by AT&T, or sold to other businesses in the form of licensing. But either way, the demands of the marketplace were a permanent part of the Unix creation environment. These realities of the business world would mix play and transgression to form a unique and unpredictable mix in the development of CBPP.

The Legitimate Businessmen's Club

On January 24, 1956, Western Electric and AT&T, the parent company of Bell Labs, signed a consent decree with the U.S. Department of Justice. This decree would mark a shift in the business culture of Bell Labs, but it would also have profound, unintended, and supremely ironic consequences for the development of Unix and its later descendents, BSD (a parallel open-source operating system) and Linux. In effect, a single corporate business decision, made on the basis of a business judgment—which could only be evaluated as prudent and conforming to sound principles of business management—would create a the most serious challenge to proprietary software in the history of computing.

AT&T was in the telephone business. In the 1950s, it was essentially licensed by the U.S. government to act as the sole provider for the nation's telephone needs. The length and breadth of Ma Bell's reach was far and wide; yet AT&T's position as the sole source of all telephone service in the United States depended upon the government's fiat, allowing it to operate without any competition. Preserving, strengthening, and extending that *raison d'être* was the primary function of AT&T business management.

Thus, it would come as no surprise that when the U.S. Justice Department and Federal Trade Commission became concerned that many of AT&T's activities were not part of its primary business of providing telephone service, AT&T management was willing to comply with the wishes of the U.S. government and avoid serious legal action. In 1949, the U.S. government brought suit action against AT&T to seek its complete divestiture of Western Electric. At that time, AT&T held complete ownership over Western Electric, the sole manufacturer of telephone equipment. AT&T would allow no other phone to connect to its network. Though it took some six years to negotiate, AT&T finally concluded that no corporate activity was worth jeopardizing its governmental charter to exist as a legal telephone monopoly and signed the consent decree. That controlling portion of that decree states that "the defendant AT&T

is enjoined and restrained from engaging, either directly, or indirectly through its subsidiaries other than Western and Western's subsidiaries, in any business other than the furnishing of common carrier communications services" (DNJ 1956). AT&T lawyers took a conservative approach in developing a business policy that conformed to the consent decree. There were some exceptions, but AT&T officially wanted no involvement in any business but the telephone business. Steven Weber writes that "it was the AT&T lawyers who read the agreement essentially to mean 'no business other than phones and telegrams,' so as not to aggravate and already strained relationship with the Department of Justice. That understanding filtered up through AT&T management to become part of the company's self-understanding" (2004, 22). AT&T was to be a "legitimate" business, and any involvement with other projects threatened to the kill the proverbial fatted calf.

Further still, the consent decree specifies in section X that "the defendants are each ordered and directed to grant or cause to be granted, to any applicant who shall make written application therefore at any time or from time to time, non-exclusive licenses under all claims of any, some or all existing and future Bell System patents" (DNJ 1956). Additionally, AT&T had to sell its future patents for a nominal flat fee—a pricing structure that did not generate a continuing revenue stream. Thus, AT&T was to be in the telephone business, and if in the practice of the telephone business it happened to create any additional patentable non-telephone products, it had to sell them cheap to anyone who might ask for them. Thus, the question became, what to do with Unix?

Unix was growing rapidly. It had transformed from Ken Thompson and Dennis Ritchie's pet project into a very useful computing tool. New computers came and left at Bell Labs, and Unix was dutifully hacked to fit each new machine. By 1971, Unix was ready to release its first edition. A manual was prepared (Thompson and Ritchie 1971). In an exact parallel to the thought processes of traditional print publication, the authors of Unix found that publication of a Unix manual triggered self-reflection and peer review. Manual publication was a coming-of-age for Unix, as noted by some of the programmers who worked both on the development of Unix and the manual preparation, such as Sandy Fraser: "The fact that there was a manual, that [Doug McIlroy, a co-creator of Unix] insisted on a high standard in the manual, meant that he insisted on a high standard of every one of the programs documented" (qtd. in Salus 1994, 39). This reveals and re-emphasizes several important parallels between Unix and traditional print literacy. First, Unix is a collaborative document, very similar to a multiple corpus document such as the Bible. Each Unix contributor worked on a program, or, often, a command. Each contributor had a login, and therefore a signature. According to another Unix author, Lorinda Cherry, "the principle involved was a simple one: 'He who touched it last, owned it.'" (qtd. in Salus 1994, 41). Program authors thus had the responsibility to ensure that their program or command was functioning properly and that the underlying code was improved by his or her contribution. All alterations to the code carried the electronic signature of the editor and the obligation to truthfully represent the status of the sub-project in the manual.

In terms of CBPP, then, we have the historical root of the most elusive component for a successful project: low-cost integration. Recall that Benkler defines the necessary components of CBPP as modularization, granularity, and cheap integration, meaning that work suited for CBPP must be (1) free of sequential order, (2) flexible in scope, and (3) with widely distributed yet reliable editorial responsibilities. By creating a rule that "he who touched it last owned it," Unix developers were literally distributing editorial powers. Each author would be held responsible for edits made with his or her login. (In fact, the authors of the first Unix manual were determined in a similar manner, with "ken" for Ken Thompson, "dmr" for Dennis M. Ritchie, "jfo" for Joseph F. Osanna, Jr., and "rhm" for Robert Morris) (Salus 1994, 41). Yet just as important, the process of publishing the manual—and a healthy collaborative culture generally—instituted an expectation of high standards. No contributor wanted to be known as someone who introduced a bug into the Unix code just before manual publication. By combining these two essential features, authorship attribution and a culture of high expectations, the Unix group achieved low-cost integration.

"He who touched it last" also offers insight into the origins of the third condition of CBPP, granularization. For CBPP to succeed, one needs work that can be enlarged or reduced as needed; from the perspective of the worker, the work needs to be something to which she can contribute as little or as much as she finds compelling. A "granular" contribution to a CBPP project must remain meaningful to both the worker and the project. Unix code was being written in an environment where many people were reviewing the work and could offer fixes as large or as small as were necessary. Thus, a contribution to fix a bug could be as small as one keystroke. As the coding environment infers, though, small changes also carry weight in terms of larger responsibility for the entire project: if your one-line fix causes a problem elsewhere in the program, then your fix has created another problem in terms of integration. As the open-source coding maxim "With enough eyeballs, all bugs are shallow" explains, granularity is essential: if one person can see the fix, then that person needs to be able to contribute. The Unix development environment also created for CBPP this third and final principle.

It is worth considering, at this point, how the Unix developers met a technical characteristic that also predetermines the existence of CBPP. The Unix developers in 1971 were working on an intranet, or a small networked environment within a local group. Benkler states that the Internet, or an easily accessible, massively-distributed network, is a precondition for the emergence of successful CBPP. The Unix team's network was easily accessed by its participants, but was more ideal than today's Internet for achieving low-cost integration. Due to its size and location—within a corporate structure—it struck a balance between the need for easy exchange of information between members of the group and individual responsibility for the integration of that work. CBPP today is a much different proposition: by applying the same principle over the Internet, a project such as Wikipedia is able to capture the intelligence, creativity, and insight a millions of participants. Yet, the project struggles to find ways to make certain that the contributions of the individuals to the project are both relevant and reliable. In short, the larger the network, the greater the potential for both significance and gibberish; there is no bond between participants-as-firm as working on Unix for the same employer, and there is no involuntary electronic signature. But just after 1971, the common denominator of corporate identity was about to get stretched.

Unix contributors were achieving low-cost integration within the walls of Bell Labs. But the project was expanding beyond Bell Labs. Since Unix had its roots in Multics, and Multics had been a joint project, Unix development was no secret among the Multics veterans. Thompson and Ritchie had a good thing, and they were happy to share it with other programmers. Unix began to expand rapidly in 1974 to other institutions; as Salus records, "The office staff [at Bell Labs] was, simply, overwhelmed by the number of requests for Unix licenses" (1994, 60).

Yet Unix was not a telephone. It was not a telegraph. It was a system of code that allowed computers to run programs. Specifically, within Bell Labs, Unix was running at Bell Labs's Research and Patent department (44). When the third edition of Unix emerged in February of 1973, the manual noted that there were sixteen installations, with more expected (47). When Ken Thompson gave a presentation on Unix at an academic computing conference in the fall of 1973, and then when that paper was published in the conference proceedings that summer, a flood of requests came in. For AT&T, this caused something of a dilemma: clearly AT&T could not sell Unix as a part of its telephone or telegraph business. The only choice under the consent decree was to sell a license for Unix at a nominal (though nominal in terms of institutional money only), flat rate. Soon, a Unix users group was established, and the first institutional mailing list gives a good idea of the breadth of institutions that were interested in purchasing Unix. The list includes: Bell Telephone Laboratories, four colleges, twenty-one universities (including Case Western Reserve, Columbia, Stanford, and Harvard), the Naval Postgraduate School, The Children's Museum, The Rand Corporation, and the Oregon Museum of Science and Industry (67–68). In short, institutions of all types were interested in purchasing a Unix license, and AT&T felt as if it were bound by the consent decree to sell it to almost anyone who asked for it and paid for the license.

As long as AT&T could make the case that Unix was part of the back-end of its telephone and telegraph business, and as long as it licensed the patented technology for a nominal fee, then AT&T felt it was in compliance with the consent decree. Within AT&T management, there were varying opinions as to whether or not Unix would make a commercially viable product. But as long as potential revenue from selling Unix was less than the revenue from a nationwide telephone monopoly, there was little point in considering the sale and marketing of Unix for AT&T. Thus, whenever AT&T sold a Unix license, it included a rather strange statement that the product was sold "as is," that there would be no support, and payment was to be made in advance. As Peter Salus records, "Andy Tannenbaum, another early Unix developer, traveled to many Unix conferences. Part of Tannenbaum's standard presentation was a projector slide which described AT&T's support policy. It read: 'No advertising; No support; No bug fixes; Payment in Advance.' This slide was always greeted by wild applause and laughter" (1994, 59). That response, it would seem, meant that the Unix users were well aware of the unique historical accident that had created Unix. Here was an essential software tool, arguably worth more than the astronomically expensive machines that ran the operating system. It was born in one of the most exclusive think tanks in America, potentially outside of the reach of the government, academia, or the general public. It had been created by a monopoly that had a long record of viciously pursuing profits through the legal protection of patents, as well as the reputation of abusing its power as monopoly with almost any individual who interacted with it. Yet when it came to perhaps its most important innovation, save for the transistor, Bell Labs's hands were tied. It could not sell the product for a profit, it had to sell it to everyone who paid, and it could not interfere with it once it was released. In essence, the legal, commercial, and cultural framework that created Unix assured its status as language. Everyone in the user community needed it as a common resource; its widespread use depended upon access and consensus; and the more it was used, the more it was adapted and improved by its users. Thus, the birth of CBPP was part genius, part historical accident, part perseverance, and part triumph of the commons.

From Unix to Linux

Unix would expand further, and the history of Unix to its more famous and contemporary descendent, Linux, is the continuation of the CBPP foundation. Berkeley would become one of the primary Unix developers. In the early days of Unix development, Berkely paid its license, got the software, and then went about altering it as it saw fit. Many of Berkeley's alterations were considered valuable, and they were added to the source code by AT&T. In the fall of 1975, Ken Thompson took a sabbatical from Bell Labs at Berkeley. Soon after Berkeley began distributing its own version of Unix known as the Berkeley Software Distribution, or BSD, which included a text editor (Weber 2004, 31). During the 1980s, the forerunner to the Internet, ARPANET, was looking for a common software base for the computers running on the network; it chose Berkeley's version of Unix, 4.1 BSD, creating a new tension between AT&T and Berkeley. In 1984 the AT&T monopoly was broken up by the federal court system, setting the end to the unique status of Unix as language. AT&T created the Unix Systems Laboratory to market Unix; the price of a Unix license increased to the point where only a few large corporations and almost no universities could afford a copy.

But Berkeley was still giving it away. Recipients of BSD were to pay AT&T for a license to the portion of BSD which was AT&T code. Later, Berkeley separated the portions of BSD which it had developed on its own and attempted to write the AT&T portions of code in a clean room—that is, they would write the code with programmers who had never seen the source code, but knew what it was supposed to accomplish. By June 1991, anyone who paid $1,000 to Berkeley could have a copy of what was then called "Networking Release 2." But the BSD license was considerably more generous than AT&T's: recipients of Networking Release 2 were free to do whatever they wanted to the code, including give away free copies, as long as they kept intact the attributions of the individual software authors (Weber 2004, 42). Many firms took BSD and marketed it on their own, and in 1992 AT&T, which was in the position of selling a software package for roughly $100,000 which one could get for free elsewhere, sued Berkeley. Ultimately the solution was a settlement wherein Berkeley agreed to redevelop BSD from an earlier release. In 2005, the BSD project has forked several times, but it remains a robust, free, and reliable Unix-like operating system.

At about the same time AT&T entered the software market with gusto, an MIT graduate named Richard Stallman composed the GNU (GNU's Not Unix) manifesto in reaction to the proprietary environment surrounding Unix (Wayner 2000, 33). Stallman was particularly decisive in his views about source code. The document spells out clearly the belief that access to modify and redistribute source code is a fundamental right; barring individuals from doing so is much akin to the idea of barring them from altering language. Furthermore, the GNU project included a new form of licensing. There is much to discuss about the license, but for the purposes of examining the fundamentals of CBPP to develop better writing strategies, it is perhaps easiest to employ the term copyleft. When ideas and expressions are placed in copyright, the copyright owner can exclude others from accessing them. When software is developed under the GNU public license, or copylefted, it becomes permanently non-copyrightable. Furthermore, others are free to take and use code developed under the GNU license, but if even a small portion of the GNU-licensed software is included in the project, then the entirety of the code falls under the GNU copyright (which is why detractors consider this arrangement a virus, and not a license).

The next stage became the most famous iteration of CBPP. On October 5, 1991, a computer science student in Finland named Linus Torvalds posted a message to a Usenet group dedicated to a Unix-like operating system named MINIX. Torvalds had written a new version of the MINIX kernel on top of many of the tools available from Stallman's Free Software Foundation. Torvalds invited anyone who was interested to take the code and do with it what they wished: "This is a program for hackers by a hacker. I've enjouyed [*sic*] doing it, and somebody might enjoy looking at it and even modifying it for their own needs" (Torvalds). Interest in the project grew and soon Torvalds placed it under the GNU copyleft license, or GPL. This meant that whenever someone added code to the Linux project, it was forever attached to Linux, and could not be sold. Not too much later, other programmers added a graphical user interface and Linux took off, with copies spreading worldwide as the functionality of the Web increased. By 2000, Linux was the most popular nonproprietary operating system in the world, with multiple distributions freely available. Linux serves as the single largest and most influential CBPP project.

Collaboration and Laziness

If collaboration was a necessary condition in the world of early modern computing, why has it persisted—even accelerated—in the era of cheap, powerful, and abundant computers? There are multiple theories to explain why collaboration has continued long after the hardware limitations were removed. One theory advanced by the more zealous advocates of open-source software, the most prominent CBPP phenomenon in the realm of software development, is that collaboration is a natural ideological choice, that people prefer to work together rather than alone, and that business and legal frameworks that seek to impede collaboration are a prima facie violation of a fundamental aspect of human nature (see Stallman 1999). Conversely, those who support proprietary models of software development often assert that collaboration in open-source software is a natural grouping of people who, for whatever reason, were not able to get their work released in the business world as individuals—that is, the work product of voluntary collaboration was not commercial grade (see Mundie 2001). More compelling, perhaps, is the political economy theory of the commons, or a resource open to everyone, which no user can deplete and most users can improve. Put more simply, no one wants to spend time repeating unnecessary work.

The computing community has burned a great amount of energy on this topic. Often, the community recasts the discussion in terms of "laziness," attracting more attention to the discussion by apparently claiming, with pride, a vice. In truth, discussions on "laziness" point up the silent slur against collaborative work as unreliable and un-virtuous—a violation of the Protestant work ethic and the notion of individual authority so ingrained in the practice of capitalism. In the self-published *Picking Up Perl*, Bradley M. Kuhn redefines "laziness" as a virtue when he writes that "lazy programmers do not like to write the same code more than once. Thus, a lazy programmer is much more likely to write code to be reusable and as applicable in as many situations as possible" (2002). Larry Wall, author of many open-source programs, as well as the founder of the Perl scripting language and community, frames this concept in controversial diction, employing a master analogy of comparing machine language to human language—when he writes that "the three great virtues of programming are laziness, impatience, and hubris. . . . Written languages probably began with impatience. Or laziness." Wall's point is that computing code, like human language, identifies and defines a community out of necessity; in order to be merely reasonably productive, a programmer cannot continually recreate a programming environment. She or he needs to work with a set of tools that reasonably can be expected to be work in other people's machines; she or he needs to write in a language her readers understand. Thus, the virtue of "laziness": early programmers such as Thompson collaborated to define a common operating environment in Unix for all programmers. Wall continues to draw this virtue in terms of a larger comparison to language: "Without written languages, you had to meet another person face to face to communicate with them . . . but written language gave people symbols, symbols that could stand for things—if the community could agree on what the symbols stood for. So language requires consensus. . . . It is, in short, a symbol that ties a community together" (127).

Pekka Himanen contributes to the development of this theme in *The Hacker Ethic* (2001). In that volume, Himanen's text is sandwiched between the contributions of Linus Torvalds, the originator of Linux, and Manuel Castells, the author of the influential and comprehensive book *The Information Age*, and Himanen's overall contribution to the concept of "laziness" as a virtue is treated by all three authors as something of a counterstatement to the concept of the Protestant work ethic. Himanen, Torvalds, and Castells would all agree with Wall that the computer-programmer mentality leads to collaboration to build a common set of tools, but expands the concept of "laziness" in ways that invoke Benkler's CBPP definition. In sum, *The Hacker Ethic* holds that the idea of workers reporting to a specific place, at a specific time, to perform a job specified by another person, has died. It has been replaced (or is being replaced) by the hacker's work ethic, where people work when they want, where they want, and only on projects that appeal to them. "Laziness," here, means that individuals work only when their creativity is piqued. Obviously, Himanen's text cannot maintain that this work arrangement is the standard arrangement; most economies are based on the capitalist model. However, Benkler's CBPP goes a long way toward examining more realistically how the modern workplace, in the age of massive networks, has shifted the working environment to expose the fact that the truest scarce resource is human creativity. In turn, Benkler's CBPP integrates the misnomer of "laziness" toward explaining the motivations for open-source software contributors: many people who do not find their creative potential fulfilled in traditional work environments elect to spend their own time working on projects that hold more interest for them.

Ken Thompson's motivation for framing Unix as a collaborative project was simply to avoid repeating unnecessary work. Unix was to be a set of common tools that Thompson and others at Bell Labs could use as a basis for their individual projects. Thus, Thompson's choice to collaborate in the creation of Unix, or his choice to work "lazily" on Unix and structure his environment so that he could dedicate more time toward work he found engaging, became a fundamental principle of Unix. Much later, it would become obvious that self-selection of work was also a fundamental principle of open source and CBPP.

Should Writing Teachers Concern Themselves with "Laziness"?

Writing teachers should concern themselves with "laziness" if and only if their students will write in environments where their writing is modular, granular, independent, and freely exchanged over the World Wide Web. In short, yes. The persistence of this massively networked electronic writing environment requires nothing short of a reassessment of the five canons of rhetoric. Invention, Arrangement, Style, Memory, and Delivery might soon include categories such as project assessment (deciding which projects a writer wishes to contribute towards, or which is "laziest") or integration (evaluating the work of yourself and others in terms of the project's needs).

In terms of understanding Unix as the root of all CBPP, and then the relationship of CBPP to teaching writing through "laziness," it is essential to understand Thompson's creation of Space Travel not only as game design, but more broadly as an expression of writing fiction. Thompson was envisioning a fictional space flight, and his means of performing that fiction was writing code. Thompson could have easily chosen a different medium—human-readable language—but he preferred instead to work with machine-readable language. Computer code gives his project a distinctively different rhetorical description than that of prose fiction, but the difference in methods does not alter the goal of placing the audience in the position of imagining space flight. The rhetoric of Space Travel still employs a writer/speaker (Thompson), a text/speech (Space Travel), and a reader/audience (player). Rather, the more significant change introduced by Space Travel is the way Thompson and others would treat the underlying code that made it possible.

In a first comparison of video game to text, and the manner in which the video game alters the more familiar rhetoric of text, we are easily drawn to the differences between roles: Is a gamer like or unlike a reader? Should we really consider a video game on the same level as text? Does a coder write for the machine or the human audience? These immediate contrasts capture the mind's eye, to be certain, and the rhetorical comparisons between coding and writing have been entertained elsewhere (cf. Cummings 2006).

But, the historical fact of the development of Unix and open source suggests some conclusions that carry over to the teaching of writing most readily. First, the comparison of the game to text masks a deeper reality: the coder's role is more like that of an author of drama, who writes a play that is then performed (cf. Juul 2005). As the author of Space Travel, Thompson created a visual rendering of space flight, which players then perform during each game. The underlying code remains unchanged, yielding performance after individual performance as players interact with the fixed text through the endlessly recursive structure of the game.

More important is what Thompson did with the underlying operating system code: he shared it and invited revisions. Recall that Space Travel is an application that functions on a computer only through the grace of the operating system environment. Thompson, as the author not only of Space Travel, but of Unix, Space Travel's (eventual) underlying operating system, invited others to collaborate on that operating system code. Thus, the text of Space Travel, endlessly performed by multiple readers, was positioned on top of code that was itself thoroughly revised. The parallel for the teaching of writing is that not only does the text exist when performed by the audience, and that each of those performances is a unique interaction between player and game (or reader and text), but also that the fundamental framework that permits the text—language— is shared and revisable by author and reader alike. This understanding— a fundamental principle of rhetorical study—guarantees fluidity in both the creation and interpretation of language. But, linguistic changes in language are glacial in pacing, whereas electronic alterations to operating system code are often immediate. Given this platform of instability, writing must then be taught from the perspective of collaboration, not only in acknowledgment of the fundamental realities of language and text but also of the history of Unix and open source. The fundamental environment of textual creation is electronic, and the text of electronic environments not only makes meaning through collaborations between authors and readers, but its electronic platform is subject to constant revision as well. Thus, the platform is inherently drawn into the web of writing: writing cannot be taught as if it was independent of the electronic environment, nor without an informed awareness of that environment's demand that we understand collaboration on a new level. Collaboration began at the level of the operating system, then moved up inexorably through the texts that its word processors have created.

If software developers, even those from competing institutions, can mutually benefit from a shared code base that they then develop on individual paths, then collaboration makes sense for all of the parties involved. Development of utilitarian blocks of code, that perform one particular task and are then shelved in a joint library to be removed and reassembled by other programmers, is a concept known as object-oriented programming, a key concept of modern computing.

A deliberate focus on collaboration eventually led to the Unix philosophy statement, in which we can find the origins of one of the key components of CBPP as defined by Benkler: modularization, which simply means that workers do not need to wait on another person to complete a task before starting their own contribution. Thus, work is "modular" if it can be broken into discrete components that do not depend on sequence for completion. Around 1973, Unix programmer Doug McIlroy summarized the Unix philosophy: "The Unix philosophy: Write programs that do one thing and do it well; Write programs that work together; Write programs that handle text streams, because that is a universal interface" (Salus 1994, 53). The CBPP concept of modularization is in both the first and second principles. Having a clearly-defined goal of "doing one thing" is a necessary precondition of modularization. Development of discrete components does not preclude "working well" together; in fact, just the opposite is true. For work to be modular, it must eventually be interchangeable. And interchangeability rests on collaborative work.

As the history of Unix and open source shows, the operating systems and software that permit writing in electronic environments are products of collaboration, a group writing project. If writing is created in the electronic environment, then it is necessarily shaped or imprinted with collaborative realities, as the tools of electronic text creation mimic the vision of the environment's creators. As composition teachers, we are just beginning to understand that electronic texts are inherently collaborative ventures, dissolving the understanding of writer as fixed and static.

While CBPP and wikis are the easiest examples of multiple-author, multiple-reader texts, their flexibility and instability are not necessarily fixed choices but rather the inevitable products of the revised and infinitely revisable code that created them. Wikis, and CBPP, force us to address the instability of language not only as it has been envisioned by linguists and postmodernists but as the logical product of the evolving electronic environment that creates electronic text.

It is difficult to overstate the role of Linux in defining CBPP. Before Linux, no one had conceived of a massive and intricate project for software that would be conducted almost entirely over a distributed network. Once Linux took shape, however, it allowed—if not required—us to reassess what is possible within information technology and electronic writing. Projects like Linux have paved the way for more traditionally prose-bound CBPP projects such as Wikipedia, which in turn has fulfilled the promise of CBPP for nontechnical but informational projects. Now that CBPP has filtered down even further to the level of social networks such as MySpace and Facebook, it is a challenge only to the imagination to envision what area of writing it will affect next.

Conclusion: Digibabble Digested

An otherwise prescient writer crafted a telling article in 1999 for *Forbes ASAP* magazine. The writer was Tom Wolfe, and the subject was nothing less broad than the Internet. There are bombasts aplenty in that article, but the one that is perhaps the most regrettable is "I hate to be the one who brings this news to the tribe, to the magic Digikingdom, but the simple truth is that the Web, the Internet, does one thing. It speeds up the retrieval and dissemination of information, messages, and images, partially eliminating such chores as going outdoors to the mailbox or the adult bookstore, or having to pick up the phone to get ahold of your stockbroker or some buddies to shoot the breeze with. That one thing the Internet does, and only that. All the rest is Digibabble" (218).

There is certainly some truth in Wolfe's perspective. Or at least there was some truth perhaps in 1999; at that point, most of the traffic on the Internet was downloaded, if not in technical terms, certainly in cultural terms. That is to say, we thought of the Internet as a device we could use to grab the same types of media we knew from an era before the Internet. We had no reason to think of the Internet as a vehicle that would change the types of things we reached for. In 1999, there were few examples of media that the Internet had specifically created.

The change from a model of the Internet based strictly on download-ing to a downloading *and* uploading model has been gradual, but it is irreversible. What has been recently called "Web 2.0" is also the official "next big thing." Beyond the hype—and there is enough hype to start pundits talking of another Internet bubble—there are a few principles that teachers of writing should observe from this latest shift.

The first principle is that students need the support of teachers to learn from networked writing environments. Wikis have played a large role in "flipping the switch" in moving the Internet from strictly a download model to a bi-directional experience. Soliciting content from almost everyone has, almost paradoxically, yielded a genuine resource. We can learn a lot from the way a Wikipedia creates knowledge, but to learn from it, we need to support our students as they explore it. The firm model of economic production reveals the fallacy of attempting to play the role of the audience for our student writers. Teachers now have the option of allowing a large and diversified audience to respond to student writing, and there can be little doubt that as more CBPP models are developed, the number of ways to allow that audience into our classes will also increase. Therefore, part of the mission of this book has been to illuminate the underlying concepts of CBPP as a writing experience so that we can see them when the next Wikipedia is developed.

A second principle is that what happens inside college writing classes need not be disconnected from CBPP: all of the laudable goals of a liberal arts education can be strengthened by conducting them in a CBPP environment. Our students will live in a world with CBPP, or more simply put, a world of networked writing. This book has attempted to look at Wikipedia as but one important instance of CBPP. Whether or not we find CBPP to be palatable as a reliable source of knowledge, and whether or not Benkler is correct in positioning it as a third economic phenomenon, there is little doubt that our students come to our writing classes familiar with networked writing, if by no other means than Facebook and MySpace. It is also true that they will leave our classes and write in a networked world. We already have a strong knowledge base for this environment. Works such as Bruffee's *Collaborative Learning* have clearly documented the mental framework—foundationalism and anti-foundationalism—we need for understanding the kinds of epistemological changes that CBPP portends.

A third principle is that there will be more collaboration to develop a theoretical understanding of how CBPP affects writing and epistemology, and rhetoric and composition theory are well-positioned to lead our understanding. It is my hope that this book will help further that process. As we continue the transformation into an information economy, rhetoric takes on an increasingly important role. Just as economics developed and adapted to explain the rules of material production in an industrial age, so too does electronic rhetoric develop to explain the rules of production in the information age. Epistemic rhetoric predicts the rules and foundation for collaboration in information networks, such as wikis, just as managerial economics predicts and explains motivations, behaviors, and rules for producing, predicting, and tracking material production.

I recently spoke with a colleague who had returned from leading a study abroad experience in London, England. I asked him how the trip had gone; as he is a veteran of both international travel and study abroad, I am always interested in learning from his experience as much as possible. He was enthusiastic about his students' experience in England, but he did note one particular irritation. "Bob," he said, "I would take them to Shakespeare's Globe, Westminster Abbey, and Trafalgar Square, and I could hardly get them to look up from their laptops long enough to note where they were." Most of these times, his students were writing e-mails, visiting Facebook, or perhaps looking for sites with more information about London, and we spoke of how these media were the new version of postcards.

It is now more than a cliché to speak of how our students live in a networked world. My friend was wise enough to recognize that, in their way, his students were indeed relating their experiences of London back to others, but his annoyance sprang from the feeling that they were missing out on "the real thing." Of course, we discussed how this situation was a classical "both and" rather than "either or": students busily writing about seeing London on electronic networks did indeed miss out on some "real" experiences, but the process of writing about experiences to friends on electronic networks made them "real" in other important ways.

Our current generation of students needs the study of network rhetoric not only because we, as their teachers, need to know how the world is creating knowledge, but also because it is this methodology of knowledge creation that they will need to use to solve the pernicious problems of the future. Consider global warming. CBPP is perhaps uniquely suited to assist in solving a tragedy of the commons since it enhances both awareness of one's station in a network as well as empathy for others in that network. The only sure way to stop a tragedy of the commons is to change the overarching economic dynamic that rewards individuals for behaviors that are destructive to themselves and others. But training a worldwide system of global capitalism to recognize environmental impact will not happen without empathy, and without the realization that indeed, just as the Internet forms a network for interconnected communications, it too forms the basis of shared awareness necessary for making visible the connection between one person's economic actions and another's environmental reality.

In *The Rise and Fall of English*, Robert Scholes attempts to describe the challenges that face the teaching of English. His book is not particularly concerned with developments in electronic rhetoric, but his grasp of the challenges that face our discipline is prescient. His work focuses not only on the developments outside the academy that threaten the status quo but on the inadequacy of our response and its historical origins. In describing his own personal conversion experience to the power of literature, he writes about seeing Arthur Miller's *Death of a Salesman*; being a fan of that play, with my own personal conversion experience as well, I find it fitting to close with Scholes's insight on both our love for teaching writing and reading as well as the challenges that we face teaching in an electronic, postmodern world:

> I had been dispatched from New Haven to see whether this new work could indeed meet the exacting academic standard for "true tragedy." I cannot remember the verdict on that count, but the play shook me down to my shoes, because it represented a business and family life so close to my own experience that it drove me to face, however briefly, the actual conditions and possibilities of my own existence. More than any other single experience, it changed me and started me down a path I have since followed. A conversion experience indeed—an experience, though, that revealed not a convergence between my literary training and the business world but a terrifying divergence of values. This gap, between the values of the humanities and those powerful worlds of business and public life, has only increased in the decades since *Death of a Salesman*

appeared. And our inability to deal with it has been a contributing cause to our present state of confusion. (1998, 18)

This book has considered the act of inviting students to write in a networked environment as an economic, rhetorical, epistemological, and pedagogical act of composing. But the predicament that Scholes describes—one of particular interest to those of us in English studies—provides one last consideration for the merits of teaching writing in a CBPP environment. If we ask our students to write in the public space provided by CBPP, not only do we return to Aristotle's vision of rhetoric as an act of public engagement, but we might also begin to close the gap that Scholes describes. The future of our students' writing lives will no doubt include wikis and CBPP, and there is little cause beyond our current practices not to accommodate these changes now.

What will networked writing look like in the future? Wikipedia's run as the premier, category-defining wiki already shows signs of change. It is difficult to envision what CBPP projects on other platforms will look like. Jimmy Wales's Wikia, Larry Sanger's Citizendium, and Google's Knol project all represent forks in the development path of the wiki. But they also represent the fundamental viability of the underlying concept of commons-based peer production. With the addition of more instances of platforms for collaboration, it becomes apparent that they are simply adding to the variety and depth of the available networks and adding to the need for understanding what motivates writers to work in collaborative environments.

References

Alchian, Armen, and Harold Demsetz. 1972. "Production, Information Costs, and Economic Organization." *American Economic Review* 62:777–95.

Bannock, Graham, R. E. Baxter, and Evan Davis. 2003. *The Economist Dictionary of Economics*. New Jersey: Bloomberg.

Benkler, Yochai. 2002. "Coase's Penguin, or Linux and the Nature of the Firm." *Yale Law Journal* 112, no. 3 (December): 369–447.

———. 2006. *The Wealth of Networks: How Social Production Transforms Markets and Freedom*. New Haven: Yale University Press.

Berlin, James A. 1987. *Rhetoric and Reality: Writing Instruction in American Colleges, 1900–1985*. Carbondale: Southern Illinois University Press.

Bizzell, Patricia, and Bruce Herzberg. 2001. *The Rhetorical Tradition: Readings from Classical Times to the Present*. 2nd ed. Boston: Bedford/St. Martin's.

Black, John. 2002. *A Dictionary of Economics*. 2nd ed. New York: Oxford University Press.

Borland, John. 2007. "See Who's Editing Wikipedia—Diebold, the CIA, a Campaign." *Wired.com*, August 14.

Bolter, Jay David. 2001. *Writing Space: Computers, Hypertext, and the Remediation of Print*. 2nd ed. Mahwah, NJ: Lawrence Erlbaum.

Bruffee, Kenneth. 1999. *Collaborative Learning: Higher Education, Interdependence, and the Authority of Knowledge*. 2nd ed. Baltimore: Johns Hopkins University Press.

Castells, Manuel. 2000. *The Rise of the Network Society*. 2nd ed. Oxford: Blackwell Publishers.

Cohen, Noam. 2007. "A History Department Bans Citing Wikipedia as a Research Source." *New York Times*, February 21. *www.nytimes.com*.

Cooke, Daniel, Joseph Urban, and Scott Hamilton. 1999. "Unix and Beyond: An Interview with Ken Thompson." *Computer* 32, no. 5 (May): 58–64. *www.computer.org*.

Corbett, Edward P. J., and Robert J. Connors. 1999. *Classical Rhetoric for the Modern Student*. 4th ed. New York: Oxford University Press.

Corbett, Edward P. J., Nancy Myers, and Gary Tate. 2000. *The Writing Teacher's Sourcebook*. 4th ed. New York: Oxford University Press.

Cummings, Robert E. 2006. "Coding with Power: Toward a Rhetoric of Computer Coding and Composition." *Computers and Composition* 23, no. 4 (December): 430–43.

Dawkins, Richard. 1989. *The Selfish Gene*. 2nd ed. New York: Oxford University Press.

DiBona, Chris, Sam Ockman, and Mark Stone, eds. 1999. *Open Sources: Voices from the Open Source Revolution*. Sebastopol, CA: O'Reilly.

DNJ (District Court of New Jersey). 1956. *United States of America v. Western Electric Co., Inc. and American Telephone and Telegraph Co.*, Civil Action 17-49. Text of consent decree accessed at *www.ip-wars.net*.

Ede, Lisa, and Andrea Lunsford. 1984. "Audience Addressed/Audience Invoked: The Role of Audience in Composition Theory and Pedagogy." In Corbett, Myers, and Tate 2000, 320–34.

Elbow, Peter. 2000. "Closing My Eyes as I Speak: An Argument for Ignoring Audience." In Corbett, Myers, and Tate, 335–52.

———. 1998. *Writing Without Teachers*. 2nd ed. New York: Oxford University Press.

Evans, David. 2003. "Class 1: Introduction." Presentation to a computer science class at the University of Virginia. *www.cs.virginia.edu/~evans/cs200-spring2003/lectures/lecture1.ppt*.

Faigley, Lester. 1992. *Fragments of Rationality: Postmodernity and the Subject of Composition*. Pittsburgh: University of Pittsburgh Press, 1992.

Flower, Linda S., and John R. Hayes. 1981. "A Cognitive Process Theory of Writing." *CCC* 32 (December): 365–87.

Frank, Robert H. 1988. *Passions Within Reason: The Strategic Role of Emotions*. New York: Norton.

Friedman, Thomas L. 2006. *The World Is Flat: A Brief History of the Twenty-First Century*. Updated and expanded edition. New York: Farrar, Straus, and Giroux.

Giles, Jim. 2005. "Internet Encyclopedias Go Head to Head." *Nature* 438:900–901. *www.nature.com*.

Glyn, Moody. 2001. *The Rebel Code: The Inside Story of Linux and the Open Source Revolution*. Cambridge, MA: Perseus Publications.

Gould, Eric. 2003. *The University in a Corporate Culture*. New Haven: Yale University Press.

Hafner, Katie. 2006. "Growing Wikipedia Revises Its 'Anyone Can Edit' Policy." *New York Times,* June 17. *www.nytimes.com*.

Hartwell, Patrick. 1985. "Grammar, Grammars, and the Teaching of Grammar." *College English* 47 (February): 105–27.

Havelock, Eric. 1982. *The Literate Revolution in Greece and Its Cultural Consequences*. Princeton: Princeton University Press.

Heilbroner, Robert, and Lester Thurow. 1998. *Economics Explained: Everything You Need to Know about How the Economy Works and Where It's Going*. New York: Touchstone.

Hicks, John. 1969. *A Theory of Economic History*. Oxford: Clarendon Press.

Himanen, Pekka. 2001. *The Hacker Ethic, and the Spirit of the Information Age.* New York: Random House.

Hjortshoj, Keith. 2001. *Transition to College Writing.* Boston: Bedford/St. Martin's.

Jameson, Fredric. 1990. *Postmodernism, or The Cultural Logic of Late Capitalism.* Durham: Duke University Press.

Juul, Jesper. 2005. *Half-Real: Video Games Between Real Rules and Fictional Worlds.* Cambridge: MIT Press.

Kuhn, Bradley M. 2002. *Picking Up Perl.* Edition 0.12. *www.ebb.org/PickingUpPerl.*

Lanham, Richard. 2006. *The Economics of Attention: Style and Substance in the Age of Information.* Chicago: University of Chicago Press.

Levitt, Steven D., and Stephen J. Dubner. 2005. *Freakonomics: A Rogue Economist Explores the Hidden Side of Everything.* New York: William Morrow.

Lomborg, Bjørn. 2001. *The Skeptical Environmentalist: Measuring the Real State of the World.* Cambridge: Cambridge University Press.

Marx, Karl. 1996. *Capital, Vol. 1.* Vol. 35 of *Marx-Engels Collected Works.* New York: International Publishers. (Original English publication 1887.)

McHenry, Robert. 2004. "The Faith-Based Encyclopedia." *TCS Daily*, November 15. *www.techcentralstation.com.*

Mundie, Craig. 2001. "The Commercial Software Model." Prepared text of remarks at the New York University Stern School of Business, May 3. *www.microsoft.com.*

North, Douglass C. 2003. "Markets." *The Oxford Encyclopedia of Economic History.* Vol. 3, ed. Joel Mokyr. New York: Oxford University Press.

O'Hare, Frank. 1973. *Sentence Combining: Improving Student Writing Without Formal Grammar Instruction.* Urbana: NCTE.

Ong, Walter J. 1975. "The Writer's Audience Is Always a Fiction." *PMLA* 90 (January): 9–21.

Paré, Anthony. 2000. "Writing as a Way into Social Work: Genre Sets, Genre Systems, and Distributed Cognition." In *Transitions: Writing in Academic and Workplace Settings*, edited by Patrick Dias and Anthony Paré, 145–66. Cresskill, NJ: Hampton.

Patton, Michael Quinn. 1990. *Qualitative Evaluation and Research Methods.* 2nd ed. Newbury Park, CA: Sage Publications.

Putterman, Louis, and Randall S. Kroszner. 1996. *The Economic Nature of the Firm: A Reader.* Cambridge: Cambridge University Press.

Reiss, Edward. 1997. *Marx: A Clear Guide.* Chicago: Pluto Press.

Ritchie, Dennis M. 1984. "The Evolution of the Unix Time-Sharing System." *AT&T Bell Laboratories Technical Journal* 63 (October): 1577–93. Available at *cm.bell-labs.com/cm/cs/who/dmr/hist.html.*

———. 1998/2001. "Space Travel: Exploring the Solar System and the PDP-7." *www.cs.bell-labs.com/who/dmr/spacetravel.html.*

———. 2001. "Ken, Unix, and Games." *ICGA Journal* 24, no. 2 (June): 67–70.

Robbins, Lionel. 1932. *An Essay on the Nature and Significance of Economic Science.* London: Macmillan.

Sanger, Larry. 2004. "Why Wikipedia Must Jettison Its Anti-Elitism." *Kuro5shin: Technology and Culture, from the Trenches*, December 31. *www.kuro5hin.org.*

Salus, Peter H. 1994. *A Quarter Century of UNIX*. Reading, MA: Addison-Wesley.

Scholes, Robert. 1998. *The Rise and Fall of English: Reconstructing English as a Discipline*. New Haven: Yale University Press.

Seigenthaler, John. 2005. "A False Wikipedia 'Biography.'" *USA Today*, November 30.

Sommers, Nancy. 1982. "Responding to Student Writing." CCC 32 (May): 148–56. Reprinted in *Teaching Writing: Theories and Practices*, ed. J. Travers. Glenview, IL: Scott Foresman, 1988.

Stallman, Richard. 1999. "The GNU Operating System and the Free Software Movement." In DiBona, Ockman, and Stone, 53–70.

Thompson, K., and D. M. Ritchie. 1971. *Unix Programmer's Manual*. 1st ed. *cm.bell-labs.com/cm/cs/who/dmr/1stEdman.html*.

Torvalds, Linus Benedict. 1991. "Free minix-like kernel sources for 386-AT." *comp. os.minix*, October 5. Accessed at *groups.google.com*.

VDS. 2007. MIT Vehicle Design Summit 2.0—Executive Summary. *vehicledesignsummit.org*.

Wall, Larry. 1999. "Dilligence, Patience, and Humility." In DiBona, Ockman, and Stone, 127–48.

Wayner, Peter. 2000. *Free for All: How Linux and the Free Software Movement Undercut the High-Tech Titans*. New York: HarperBusiness.

Weber, Max. 1958. *The Protestant Ethic and the Spirit of Capitalism*. Translated by Talcott Parsons. New York: Scribner.

Weber, Steven. 2004. *The Success of Open Source*. Cambridge: Harvard University Press.

"Wikipedia Epidemic." 2005. UGA English department discussion list, March 17. *www.listserv.uga.edu*.

Wilkinson, Nick. 2005. *Managerial Economics: A Problem-Solving Approach*. New York: Cambridge University Press.

Williams, Alex. 2008. "The Falling-Down Professions." *New York Times*, January 6. *www.nytimes.com*.

Wolfe, Tom. 1999. "Digibabble, Fairy Dust, and the Human Anthill." *Forbes ASAP*, October 4: 213–17.

Yancey, Kathleen Blake, and Irwin Weiser, eds. 1997. *Situating Portfolios: Four Perspectives*. Logan: Utah State University Press.

Index

Page numbers in bold indicate illustrations.

DATE DUE

FEB 16 2013

SEP 2 3 REC'D

SEP 2 3 REC'D